Matricide in Language

Matricide in Language
WRITING THEORY IN KRISTEVA AND WOOLF

MIGLENA NIKOLCHINA

OTHER

Other Press
New York

Copyright © 2004 Miglena Nikolchina

Production Editor: Robert D. Hack

This book was set in 11 point Berkeley by Alpha Graphics of Pittsfield, NH.

10 9 8 7 6 5 4 3 2 1

Library of Congress Cataloging-in-Publication Data

Nikolchina, Miglena.
  Matricide in language : writing theory in Kristeva and Woolf / by Miglena Nikolchina.
    p. cm.
Includes bibliographical references and index.
  ISBN 1-59051-080-1 (pbk. : alk. paper)
  1. Kristeva, Julia, 1941—Criticism and interpretation. 2. Woolf, Virginia, 1882–1941—Criticism and interpretation. I. Title.
  PN75.K75 N55 2003
  801'.95'082—dc22

                                                2003022545

To Joan Scott

Contents

Acknowledgments

A grant from the Institute for Advanced Study, Princeton, New Jersey, gave me the chance to complete my work on this book. I owe gratitude to Joan Scott for her unwavering support and to Judith Butler for her encouragement and fruitful suggestions. Discussions with Elizabeth Harvey, Kristin Brady, and John Graham helped me at the earlier stages of my work. Last but not least, my special thanks to Tania Roy for her delicate reading and corrections of the manuscript.

Introduction: Matricide and Language

The nexus of psychoanalytic, literary, and philosophical approaches in this book focuses on an intertextual reading of Virginia Woolf and Julia Kristeva. Its goal is to address the enigma of the persistent depletion of women's contributions to culture. The claim that emerges is that, in spite of the huge efforts of feminist theory and history to turn the tide, this process is with us still. Its tenacity can be illustrated through the history of centuries of attempts to remove Diotima, the wise priestess who offers the crucial speech in Plato's dialogue the *Symposium*, from the site of the birth of Western philosophy. As David Halperin (1990) put it, "Depleted by Socrates, [Diotima] vanishes, but Socrates's erotic wisdom and his entrancing speeches endure" (p. 148). Diotima vanishes because of Socrates's speeches? Because of Plato's writings? Or because of Platonic commentary and its strange need to retroject the vanishing of Diotima at the very place of her appearance?

The intertextual approach to Kristeva and Woolf will bring to light "matricide" as the silent engine behind this vanishing, which is not a given but which is constantly resumed. The reason we do not heed sufficiently this constantly resumed vanishing process; the reason we can even afford to assert the redundancy of theory for addressing the problems of women, problems, presumably, that are always reducible to the mundane and the everyday, is the specific cunning of the depletion. The maleness of all wisdom with its entrancing speeches is a retroactive phenomenon: it produces the illusion that the present, any present, is always far more generous than the past in terms of its recognition of women's names. The past was unfair, the present is full of promise, and the future will set things right. The driving force behind this perennial optimism is the work of forgetfulness.

"I am the first of a new genus" (Mary Wollstonecraft). "When I looked around, I saw and heard of none like me" (Mary Shelley). "I look everywhere for grandmothers and find none" (Elizabeth Barrett Browning). "Why isn't there a tradition of the mothers?" (Virginia Woolf). Women have "no past, no history" (Simone de Beauvoir). "I look for myself throughout the centuries and I don't see myself anywhere" (Hélène Cixous).[1] As Woolf (1958) noted, "strange spaces of silence" (p. 77) separate the solitary female utterances throughout history. The brutal vicissitudes of the contemporary reception of feminist thinkers, so carelessly read and so prematurely dismissed, the repeated waves of resentment with feminist theory, crushed between the traditional academia and a "misosophy" that describes itself as activism, the war waged on the so-called French feminists who, unlike their male counterparts, have been persistently marginalized on the American scene, the attacks on "difficult" writing from the platform of an anti-intellectualism that all women are supposed to crave—all these are symptoms of the fact that the conditions that produced the "strange spaces of silence" and made the repetitive generic loneliness from Wollstonecraft to Cixous possible are still operative. They have found their way into the present age "reactionary conformity that manages to discredit any notion of feminine specificity or freedom that is not based on seduction—which means not based on reproduction and consumption" (Kristeva 2001a, p. xiii).

MATRICIDE

In the hope of uncovering the structural dimensions of what is, in effect, a diachronic phenomenon, I turned to Julia Kristeva's interdisciplinary study

---

1. I return to these statements in Chapter 4.

of the figure of the mother. Beginning with *Powers of Horror* (1982; published in French in 1980), Kristeva's explorations of the maternal figure repeatedly return to the problem of the phantasmatic matricide as the necessary condition of individuation. Since, in phantasy, separation and loss appear as death, the most fundamental psychic problem that the would-be speaking being has to solve—separation from the archaic mother—appears as murder. Kristeva evolves this problematic out of Melanie Klein, in whom, paradoxically, the cult of the mother is transformed into an imaginary matricide. "The loss of the mother—which for the imaginary is tantamount to the death of the mother—becomes the organizing principle for the subject's symbolic capacity" (Kristeva 2001b, pp. 129–130). The necessity of matricide faces the would-be speaking being as the only way toward subjectivity and language.

There is something drastically irrevocable about this necessity that "both sexes share" (Chasseguet-Smirgel 1989, p. 25, Wieland 2000, pp. 13–14). The extreme nature of matricide is emphasized by the impossibility of incorporation or integration of the murdered mother (in the way the father, in Freud, is incorporated by the murderous brothers through eating the totem). Matricide, on the contrary, is realized as rejecting or even "vomiting" the maternal body. This rejection—out of which the *abject* with its powers of horror will be formed—draws the first boundary between inside and outside, it is the first line separating a still fragile "I" from an "everything else." "I feel like vomiting the mother" (Kristeva 1982, p. 47): this metaphor of ungiving birth to the mother against the stream of time names an archaic creative act that establishes the first boundary, the first precarious measurement of space, and the primal irrecoverable loss.

"Fear of the archaic mother turns out to be essentially fear of her generative power. It is this power, a dreaded one, that patrilineal filiation has the burden of subduing" (Kristeva 1982, p. 77). "Phallic power, in the sense of a symbolic power that thwarts the traps of penial performance, would in short begin with an appropriation of archaic maternal power" (Kristeva 1987b, p. 75). And: "Phallic idealization is built upon the pedestal of a putting-to-death of the feminine body" (Kristeva 1987b, p. 357). The concept of "matricide" uncovers the dark lining of Gilbert and Gubar's (1988) concepts of anxiety of authorship and female affiliation complex, which they set against Harold Bloom's (1973) anxiety of influence. There is no symmetry between patricide and matricide. Patricide produces lineage; matricide is perpetuated as erasure of the "name of the mother."

THE LANGUAGE OF POETS IS ALWAYS A DEAD LANGUAGE

The poet and the thinker of the void have a privileged access to the awareness that the "Mothers are dead" (Agamben 1999, p.74). The psychoanalytic perspective, however, offers access to a knowledge that both poetry and philosophy try to short-circuit: the knowledge that, in language, the mother is not simply dead but murdered, and that the murder has gendered repercussions for the speaking subject. Kristeva's elaboration of this psychoanalytic access involves the methodological mobilization of two opposing poles. On the one hand, there is the exploration of "the practice of the rebel subjectivity which allows the individual to live at the frontiers of pleasure and death and society to transcend its necessary limits" (Kristeva 2002b, p. 7). The "rebel subjectivity" summons the figure of the poet, the artist, the deviser of new territories and new languages, the producer and reconstructor of culture. On the other hand, there is the study of the "space vis-à-vis reason," requiring the frameworks of different disciplines: linguistics and poetics, psychoanalysis and semiotics, epistemology and metaphysics, anthropology and the histories of art, religion, or political ideas. This joining of theory and art in search for the "dead mother" aims at uncovering the dynamic factor in both the generation and the transgressive exceeding of the subject and its languages.

To describe this dynamic, Kristeva's work invokes a number of concepts (the *chora* of Plato's ontology, the *Negativität* and *Kraft* of Hegel's dialectic). Among her various attempts to name the void and its unsettling powers, the *abject* is certainly one of Kristeva's most engaging masterstrokes. Her book *Powers of Horror* (1982) introduces the abject at the crossroads of Mary Douglas's anthropological study of abjection and Freud's psychoanalytic study of phobia. It takes us to Melanie Klein's problematization of the early sadistic phantasies directed toward the interior of the maternal body, from which the primary relation to the external world will be constituted. The abject thus names the disquieting and unstable division preceding the subject-object dichotomy. The fact that the phantasmatically murdered and rejected maternal body lurks behind this concept as well as behind the "Thing" of the melancholic was often perceived as questionable from a feminist point of view. Even if we leave aside Kristeva's profound writing on the feminine—as distinct from femininity and as open-ing new vistas for our understanding of society and thinking[2]—we can see in Kristeva's work a theoretic rehabilitation of the maternal figure. The tale/history of maternal loss emerges as the destiny of the speaking being—horrified, persecuted, mournful, and therefore creative. As *abject, Thing, semiotic, chora*, the maternal void shakes and pulverizes meanings, it shat-ters and produces them. Yet it also opens a bifurcating path for the gendered speaking being and presents the lures of specific hazards for the feminine positioning in language. These lures have not bypassed the feminist dis-cursive field. The representations of this field, torn between the idealiza-tions offered by its proponents and the denigrations characteristic of its opponents, tend to screen the brutality of its inherent functioning between fusion and murder. If we address this immanent dynamic theoretically, we can, I believe, enhance our understanding of the internal and external dif-ficulties that made so many thinkers—Woolf and Kristeva included—dis-sociate themselves from feminism, and which have led to the repeated proclamation of feminism itself as dead.

KORE

Some cautious remarks are warranted before I move on: some inescapable qualifications and restrictions to the matricidal theme. It is true that, as Kristeva (2001b) points out apropos Klein, "without matricide the inter-nal object cannot be formed, the fantasy cannot be constructed, the repa-ration, as well as the redirection of the hostility into the introjection of the self, is foreclosed" (p. 130). And yet, both matricide and the cult of the mother offer salvation. Hence the necessity that "both sexes share" came through in Kristeva's theory with its halo of a lost paradise. Although throughout her work Kristeva always insisted on the presence of the third party, of the "paternal inscription" in the early stages of development, and in spite of the frequent criticism that she privileged the mother–son rela-tionship through the figure of the male artist (in her most recent writing, she has emphatically reversed this tendency), Kristeva conceptualizes the

---

2. See "Oedipus again, or Phallic Monism" and "On the Extraneousness of the Phal-lus, or the Feminine Between Illusion and Disillusion" (in Kristeva 2000a, pp. 65–106) and "Y-a-t-il un génie féminin" (in Kristeva 2002a, pp. 537–566).

early mother as a hallucinatory osmosis between mother and daughter. In an echo from Freud, she calls this figure a Minoan-Mycenaean mother. This early mother refers to a modality where the son is also a girl or—to put things once again in the language of ancient myth—a Kore, the forever lost-and-found daughter of Demeter (Fairfield 1995). In the vein of the Minoan-Mycenaean phantasmatics, therefore, of the skin-to-skin osmosis, of the in-betweenness of barely distinguishable identities, the reduplicating goddess Demeter-Kore represents an early stage of primary identification with the mother. Thus unlike the mother who is phallicized by the son and hence a mother-and-son, the Minoan-Mycenean mother is a mother-and-daughter—and an echo, perhaps, of the irrepresentable transphalic jouissance of a prelinguistic sensory fusion. Kristeva relates this aspect of her writing on maternity to Freud and distinguishes it from Klein's darker vision (Kristeva 2001b). It is worth noting at this point, however, that the prevalence of this idealization is very typical of Bulgarian folklore and Bulgarian women's literature.[3]

FEMALE LIBIDO

In *To the Lighthouse* (1927), Virginia Woolf situates the creativity of her protagonist, Lily Briscoe, under the sign of a striking convergence between the dead mother and the enticements of osmotic bliss. In a compelling transmutation of the *Symposium*, Plato's dialogue on love, the dissymmetries and inequalities, the tensions and anxieties, the violent oppositions and the agonistic extremities that characterize the master–slave dialectic of the Platonic Eros, and that surface in Freud's conceptualization of the libido, disappear into the image of liquids uniting without remnant and becoming "inextricably the same." In an intense scene with Lily Briscoe pressing against Mrs. Ramsay's knee, no words are exchanged between Mrs. Ramsay and Lily: they do not speak, they touch. Body and mind intermingled, boundaries blurred, liquid identities become indistinguishable, murmurs and stirrings dissolved in the "sharpness or sweetness" of the air: we are in the perilous and jubilatory realm of feminine erotic.

---

3. Kristeva is a Sofia University graduate and was 24 when she left Bulgaria for France. I touch upon certain "Bulgarian" aspects of the idealized maternal figure in Chapter 2.

This erotic is conceptualized in Kristeva's work as "female libido."[4] *Female libido* is a term that Kristeva evolves out of Winnicott and Klein; that is subtended (like most things in Kristeva) by the death drive; and that designates a specific type of correlation between drives and the symbolic. In the 1990s, Kristeva elaborated the idea of a "relentless fusional libido" (Kristeva 1996, p. 77) through Proust's theory of homosexuality and of the distinctiveness of Sodom and Gomorrah. Like Freud's male libido, which is common to men and women and informs any erotic relationship, the female libido is not applicable to only certain groups of people. It is an amorous space approachable from any gender position. Freud insisted that there is one libido only, male, and referred its predatory sadomasochistic dynamic to the Platonic concept of Eros. Kristeva's elaboration of female libido—which, in her latest work, she prefers to designate as an "other libido"—transforms Freud's concept in the manner in which Woolf transforms Plato's Eros. Fusional and osmotic, rather than dialectic, female libido acts as an erotization without residue that permeates the universe with an amorous glow and ushers in mystic and ecstatic merging—the Schopenhauerean relinquishment of will, the Oriental Nothingness of Nirvana.

Both libidinal economies spring from a crux of destructiveness and generation that is as yet ignorant of the dramas of sex and gender. Freud, as Kristeva (1987b) reiterates, anchors the morbid, manic, and destructive aspects of Eros "in the prehistory of matter that propagated by means of scission before having acquired an organ with erotic and procreative functions" (p. 79). Kristeva, on her part, relates the lethal, depersonalizing tendency of the "feminine erotic" to the "loving dialogue of the pregnant mother with the fruit, barely distinct from her, that she shelters in her womb" (p. 81). Violent and destructive to begin with, the male libido immediately presents to life the task for its shackling. According to Kristeva's reading of the *Symposium*, it is feminine love that becomes a mediator in the dramaturgy of male libido by providing the turning point from destruction to idealization, from pleasure to knowledge. The problem with female libido in its pure form, however, is its alluring deceptiveness: it appears as the

---

4. In her early work, Kristeva follows Freud in designating this quasi-libido as "objectless." With her later work, however, which has moved closer to Klein, the object (the breast) is there from the start and the concept of an "other libido" has become more concrete (Kristeva 2002a, p. 552).

promise of an ecstatic deathless universe. This promise then, may turn out to be the "grinding death" of the refusal of separation. Through the traps of the lost paradise, therefore, through the ecstasies of fusion that support the phantasy of a mother eternally living in the flesh, we may come back to murder. If Mrs. Ramsay is the object of Lily Briscoe's osmotic longings, then keeping Mrs. Ramsay sufficiently dead is Lily Briscoe's paradoxical problem in *To the Lighthouse*.

ABJECTIVITY AND MERGINALITY

I offer my exploration of matricide and female libido in this book as an entry into the cultural ramifications of a language that wavers between hypnotic passion and murder. In a striking account, Joan Scott (2001) presents the oscillations between phantasies of uniqueness and phantasies of fusion as characteristic of women's movements. My claim is that these phantasies are linked to the matricidal phantasmatics, and that they can explain extreme discursive practices that are characteristic of the debate in and around feminism, but that are, for sure, not restricted to this debate and can be encountered in any discursive field. Margaret Whitford (1994), who observes this phenomenon with regard to the reception of Irigaray, describes it as a vacillation between "the Scylla of idealization and the Charybdis of denigration" (p. 23).

Before I turn to the two rhetorical forms that Scylla and Charybdis assume, those mythical monsters that crushed any navigator who tried to maneuver between them, I need to introduce yet another term. The zone demarcated by the female libido has, according to Kristeva (1989), its proper language: *reduplication*. Reduplication, carried out as a "jammed repetition" (p. 246) is the direct expression and the immediate language of female libido. Referring to the outmost limits of our unstable identities, reduplication unfolds as a stammering of temporality that forever struggles to pronounce one and the same petrified moment. It is an eternal return of the same, but, unlike the return that is rippled out in time reduplication is a reverberation outside of time. It is, therefore, a spatial occurrence, yet even its spatiality is unstable and tends to collapse in a play of mirrors lacking perspective or duration. Its medium is the false space created by the play of mirrors and the reverberations of echoes, by the "hypnotic passion" that sees only doubles. It is the fathomless exploration of the same; the uncovering of the same's secret depths that threaten to engulf it.

Two distinct routes open here. Referring to Kristeva's concept of the abject, I term the first one *abjectivity*. Abjectivity is literary assassination that presupposes a baffling inattentiveness toward the texts of the author. Careless as it is about words, however, abjectivity cannot be reduced to a simple scholarly negligence since it is bent on the reading of a more diffi- cult text. A transcendental text where, on the far side of words, a faulty and culpable female body—as is the case with the frigid childless body of Woolf—is exposed before being abjected. With its monotonous produc- tion of maternal corpses, abjectivity remains trapped by a curious circu- larity: the victorious murderer appears as the forgetful replica of an earlier, supposedly lethal writing that is incorpsed and thrown out of the body proper of literature. The result is a blocking of spatial and temporal dis- creteness that dooms the writing woman to be forever the first of her kind. Or, to put it in more neutral terms, to be the lateral and contingent com- panion to the diachronic necessities of male filiation: Shakespeare's sister as Woolf imagined her in *A Room of One's Own*.

Similar results may follow from a specific kind of rhetorical technique that can be described as fusional or symbiotic, or, indeed, as osmotic *érotique du féminin*: mobilized in order to restore femininity to writing, it runs the risk of inadvertently eradicating any alterity. The voice of the author under discussion melts in the voice that discusses her in a "merginality" (with an "e") that allows no distance or difference. Since it dissolves boundaries and differences, merginality provokes the anxieties of reduplication, of "hyp- notic" sameness and hovers, precariously blissful, over the always open temptations of violence.

Murder or jouissance. Murder *and* jouissance. Whether through amo- rous fusion or through total obliteration of the adversary, both abjectivity and merginality tend to hurtle discourse outside of time. They both oc- cupy an atemporal realm where the female speaking subject emerges as a solitary presence without memory or precedents, as a forever *jeune née*. The ultimate problem with abjectivity and merginality is that they facilitate a compulsive forgetfulness that dooms a female voice to repeat incessantly its inauguration.

At this point I need to make clear that the pathos of my argument diverges from Kristeva's latest writing on the feminine and on what she defines as the female genius. Kristeva's trilogy on Hannah Arendt, Melanie Klein, and Colette presents a systematic effort to link the intellectual achievements of concrete women with a profound theory of the feminine as the very basis of sociality and of the social relation. In her conclusion to

the trilogy, Kristeva evokes Simone de Beauvoir who, in the spirit of exis-
tentialism, contrasted the constricting situation of women with the task of
the individual to realize her freedom as a human being. Kristeva's (2002a)
critique of Beauvoir is that she chose to lay the emphasis on the necessity
to change the situation of women, and so underestimated the subject of
whose value she was so well aware. And yet, Kristeva's own emphasis on
singularity, on the "irreducible subjectivity" (p. 543) of her geniuses as the
solution that can forgo the pitfalls of the "situation of women" (Kristeva
2001c, p. 119) and the impasses and dogmatisms of mass movements
cannot, and does not, attempt to challenge the bifurcation that I am trying
to address—the bifurcation between fusion and uniqueness. Kristeva's
twentieth century "female genius" (seen positively as precisely the ability
to transcend the situation) was already an issue in the nineteenth century
as "true genius, but true woman" (Gilbert and Gubar 1988, p. 211) and
contains a curious reverberation of Wollstonecraft's "new genus." Between
the awesome amassment of women's archives today and the repetitive figures of praise of female singularity, the figures of authority that inform our
thinking and through which we effect the continuity of thinking are still
male. The uniqueness/fusion bifurcation, with all the respect I feel for the
rebellious investment in singularity, cannot satisfy the ethos of dialogue
and interactive togetherness, of the irreducible collectivity of thinking,
which is the unsaid ideal behind my own take on matricide.

FROM INTERTEXTUALITY TO PERPETUUM MOBILE

The book is divided into two parts. Part I consists of three chapters and
examines but also performatively enacts Kristeva's theory of maternity on
a number of levels (from the theoretical via the fictional to the poetic).
Chapter 1 examines the theoretical aspects of Kristeva's conceptualization
of maternity and of matricide as the sine qua non of individuation. It insists on the productive and heuristic aspects of this conceptualization, which
allows a specific entrance to ontological and epistemological problems,
and to problems of subject formation. Chapter 2 explores the fictional
dimension of Kristeva's theoretical elaboration of maternity and matricide. This fictional dimension turns out to be a narrative of exile and of
an unnameable loss that can be recuperated through artistic creativity,
or through a theory conscious of its passions. It is only by *translating the
mother* that we live: "orphans but creators, creators but forsaken" (Kristeva

1989, p. 181). Chapter 3 examines the matricidal problematic against the background of the irreversible transformation of the maternal function, which technology is already bringing about. This chapter thus draws to a close the examination of the "lethal" aspects of the phantasmatic matricide in conjunction with its positive—creative—potential.

Part II also comprises three chapters. Chapters 4 and 5 offer the crux of my argument by focusing on the predominantly destructive deployment of matricide as "abjectivity" and "merginality." The figure of Diotima, the visionary priestess from the *Symposium*, emerges as emblematic of the centuries of repeated efforts to obliterate the woman who is present at the site of the birth of Western philosophy. Chapter 6 discusses Woolf's late writing (*Between the Acts* and her unfinished project on anonymity—she was thinking of the death of the author, an idea that, paradoxically but not surprisingly, is now the property of male authors who came after Woolf). Uncovering, in *Between the Acts*, a perpetuum mobile that "thinks the world into existence," this chapter interprets Woolf's "final answer" as a maternal gesture that can still offer hope to those who come before or after her.

My theoretical narrative moves from the discussion of Kristeva in the first part of the book to a blend between Kristeva and Woolf, in which there is more and more Woolf and less and less Kristeva, until finally it is Woolf who provides the answer to her own excruciating questions—the questions that made me turn to Kristeva in the first place. Kristeva's concept of intertextuality, the transformation of one sign-system into another or, rather, the overlapping interference and mutual transformation of different sign-systems, provides a fit designation for this procedure that bypasses unified space and linear chronology. *Reverberation* might be an even better term here, a term that will positivize the stammering of matricidal temporality and the blocked repetition of female libido. In Kristeva's conceptualization of female libido, reverberation is used as a process annihilating temporality and, whether positively or negatively, I also tend to use this term in an atemporal manner. Joan Scott (2002), however, has developed reverberation in conjunction with "echo" as a heuristic model that might offer a new perspective to the ways in which historicity—with regard to women but also in general—creates its continuities. "Not just a distorted repetition but also movement in space and time—history reverberations are described by Scott as "seismic shock waves moving out from dispersed epicenters, leaving shifted geological formations in their wake" (p. 11). In Woolf's last novel, *Between the Acts* (1941), the jammed repetition of a gramophone offers the image of ultimate despair but also of a "seismic" constantly interrupted space and time continuum. In this mode of reverberating space and time, Woolf, through a remarkable stroke of artistic cunning, was finally able to transform silence into lineage and interruption into a perpetuum mobile of new beginnings.

POSTREVOLUTIONARY, POSTPOETIC

There is a certain wavering in this book of which I am aware, a wavering between matricide and fusion, between horror and ecstasy. This wavering is partially my own and is insurmountable; partially, it is the reflection on a shift in the perspective in Kristeva's writing, a shift concerning not so much the conceptual aspects of her theory of matricide and its adjacent osmotic paradise, but rather the evaluative and rhetorical emphases. In her earlier work, of which *Powers of Horror* is representative, Kristeva tends to focus on the scary and dramatic aspect of the relationship to the archaic mother: to her horrifying and deadly call, that "black lava" that allures us with the temptation of simple nonbeing, dissolution, lethal fusion. Due to woman's estrangement from the symbolic (a question that I pursue in some detail throughout the book), this call is especially perilous for women: Marina Tsvetaeva who wants "not to die but not to be"; Virginia Woolf sinking silently into the river. More recently, however, Kristeva prefers to bring forth the risks that follow from the extremity of female assumptions of the phallic position. Such assumptions lead to annulment of the primary semiotic link with the mother and to a complete identification with phallic power. The emphasis is, in other words, more and more clearly— although this should have been clear from the start—on the necessity both sexes share not to murder the mother completely after all.

It is worth emphasizing at this point that the ecstatic and murderous perspective into which matricide casts the feminine is, for Kristeva, a matter of the body and of corporeality only in terms of the unnameable residue that produces the unsettling of power systems. Her concern is with the aporia of sensation, irreducible to any representation, yet dependent on it; and with the psyche as a stratified significance that the linguistic and cognitive imperialisms conceal and redistribute along the sole dimension of language. It is this hidden heterogeneity with its potential to unsettle established meanings that she explores (Kristeva 1996). What matters for her is the trajectory from the nonsignifiable body to art with its investments in the imaginary and to that "coalescence of sensations and linguistic signs that we call literary style" (p. 235), but also to love and the psychoanalytic production of literature for two. Along this trajectory, as Kristeva so many times has insisted, there lies the possibility for renewal and revolt.

It is worth, therefore, to reiterate the promise held out by the primeval maternal light as distinguishable from the threats of its "black lava." Yet the very hope for such a promise seems to grow out of a growing awareness of the bifurcation of modern experience between an unsignifiable acting out, on the one hand, and the contention of legal and political discourses, on the other. What crumbles and vanishes in the in-between is artistic production, the revolution in poetic language and, ultimately, our ability to resolve the aporia of sensation and confront in a meaningful way the irreducibility between sensation and sign. Endemic food disorders, skins that seem to be never completed and in constant need of inscription, and touching, any touching relegated to the realm of the sexual and hence to the realm of the regulated and the forbidden, seem to indicate a common disturbance in our most elemental links to our environment, itself in the grips of a sea change. Is this the beginning of the process that will finally take the chips of our motherless souls out among the stars? At the dawn of an irreversible transformation of the maternal function, a transformation that technology is already bringing about, on the verge of a civilization that has successfully sanitized the troubling continuum exemplified by the maternal body, the continuum that the maternal used to provide phantasmatically, but also in terms of material permeability with the cosmos of other living creatures, of blood and cells, of life and death, what we have to face, perhaps, are the consequences of a matricide too final, too complete.

Part I

The Polylogic Wager

The Quest for the Mother:
Theoretical Aspects of the Polylogue

At its various stages, Julia Kristeva's theoretical writing develops the problem of maternity and the figure of the mother with reference to the conceptual frameworks of different disciplines: linguistics and poetics, psychoanalysis and semiotics, epistemology and metaphysics, anthropology and the histories of art, religion, and political ideas. "Develops" should be read here in its double meaning: elaborates a concept, and makes an invisible image come through. In the latter meaning, the presumption would be that the maternal space vis-à-vis reason was always already there, within the functioning of the various discourses, but veiled. Camouflaged. Alluding to the classical myth of Zeus's swallowing of the goddess of wisdom Metis, one might say: swallowed.

To gain access to this hidden space, Kristeva's theoretical approaches turn toward other realms of signifying practices, that is, spheres of activity that exhibit the process of the sign's becoming. In their double mode of constituting and traversing the system of signs, signifying practices involve the making and the unmaking of the speaking subject and its identity. Hence they require an unfinished, splitting and fragmented, multiple and dynamic subject in the grips of pain and jouissance, which Kristeva problematizes as a subject-in-process. Artistic practice, the situation of transference, and,

least orthodoxically, the act of giving birth as the site of a split symbolization, provide their several perspectives for the always uncertain scene at
the far side of signification, whence bodies, identities, and signs are begot-
ten (Kristeva 1980).

Insofar as the mother is concerned, two major outcomes emerge out
of this joining of theory and practice. Theoretical discourse, traversed by
the signifying practices it seeks to analyze, approaches its own outer limits
and questions its own assumptions. The execution of this corrosive questioning is designated by Kristeva as semanalysis, a procedure that meets
the requirement to describe the signifying phenomenon, or signifying
phenomena, while analyzing, criticizing, and dissolving "phenomenon,
meaning, and signifier" (Kristeva 1980, p. vii). Within this setting of theory-
as-practice, the maternal space is revealed as the outside that both delineates and challenges the rigor and the coherence of theoretical homogeneity.
Confronted with the analytic venture, signifying practices, on the other
hand, wield a knowledge that they do not necessarily know but that ren-
ders the production of meaning and of the subject transparent. Through this
knowledgeable transparency, the mother is recovered as the dynamic factor in both the generation and the exceeding of the signifier. For the homogeneous space where meaning, syntax, and logic hold sway, the mother is
the outside that sustains it and exposes its limitations; within the heterogeneous space where signs are produced and dissolved, the mother is the
dialectic that generates and shatters them.

In this way, a pervasive narrative, a fiction, or, to activate the ambiguity of the French word *histoire*, a history and a tale surface across Kristeva's
theory. This is the history and the tale of the mother, of her absence (for
she is always outside of syntax and logic), and of her power (for she is their
constitutive and productive outside). This, moreover, is a history and a
tale of great pathos. It tells of the precautious loss (of the mother), of the
pains, the fears, and the longings brought about by the separation (from
the mother), and of the disconsolate wanderings (in search of the mother)
of the speaking being. An exile prone to despondency and exaltations,
s/he is destined to traverse the forever foreign country of other languages
and metalanguages that promise a reunion (with the mother), and yet de-
viate further and further away from her in a perpetual polytopic quest.

And this is not all. If the disjunction between the homogeneous and
synchronic space where theoretical codes function and the heterogeneous
and diachronic space where they come into being gives rise to the fiction
of the powerful but lost mother, there is also a mode in which synchrony

and diachrony become coextensive. Heterogeneity is set forth as part of the symbolic homogeneity itself—a transversal, wayward part, to be sure, that makes the absent mother in effect always present. This problematic presence criss-crosses the linearity of the symbolic as the order of the sign, of syntax, and of the law. Kristeva designates it as the semiotic chora. Although a precondition of the symbolic in terms of its *histoire*, although a sequence of the symbolic in terms of its organization into an observable device, the semiotic chora is always simultaneous with it as the symbolic's shaking and transgression: an excess that makes language sing, and that explodes light into color. Most evident in avant-garde poetic practice, the semiotic nevertheless inhabits and is inhabited by any functioning of language and the symbolic. It thus presents a constant challenge to temporal distinctions through the paradox of a past that never passes and that finds its reiteration as rhythm and laughter.

Kristeva's work, therefore, brings the maternal, first, into theory through the rewriting of certain concepts (the chora of Plato's ontology, the *Negativität* and *Kraft* of Hegel's dialectic); and through the persistent unsettling of the subject-object dichotomy by other, less distinct and more disquieting divisions (the abject of the abject, where the very necessity to name in one and the same way the subject and the object of abjection indicates the uncertainty of the division; the thing of the melancholic; as well as their luminous correlative in the jouissance of the mystic and the artist). Second, across this theoretic rehabilitation of the mother the tale/history of her loss emerges as the presiding destiny of the speaking being, forever mournful and therefore creative. And finally (in the logical order that I propose and not in the chronology of Kristeva's biography as an author), the semiotic smuggles in the mother as a transversality to both theory and fiction, shaking and pulverizing meanings when it is not actually shattering and producing them: as the rhythm and the exorbitance of sound in language, as the excess of color in painting, as the very principle of music or dance, and in all that as the nonsignifiable articulation of jouissance and death.

THE THEORETICAL SUBJECT

Kristeva's theoretical writing does not simply lay out all these maternal aspects of the destiny of the speaking being, but rather involves them in a signifying practice (the practice that partakes of the making and unmaking of the subject and the sign). The subject of theory is an unalienable and indispensable dimension of the theory that purports to take into account the crises of meaning, subject, and structure. Through the notion of the epistemological device, Kristeva insists on the interrelation between the subject of theory and its object. What is the epistemological device of Kristeva's theory? Is there a theoretical subject-in-process across the theory of the subject-in-process presented in *The Revolution in Poetic Language* (Kristeva 1974)? Is the theoretician of abjection in *Powers of Horror* (Kristeva 1982) a precarious subject haunted by a ghostly glimmer? Is the study of melancholy in *Black Sun* (Kristeva 1989) the painful enunciation of a melancholy theoretician? Is Kristeva's theoretician stratified across the heterogeneous polytopical space of the signifying processes that she studies? Is this theoretician a "subject in infinite analysis" (Kristeva 1980, p. 146)? Can theory be a text, that is, "the experience of a subject in history" (Kristeva 2002b, p. 6), and is it possible to adopt a perspective in which Kristeva's theoretical writing is a text? Sometimes explicitly, but in all cases by its operations, Kristeva's writing makes us face the requirement that we take into account the subject of theory as part of the theory itself.

This requirement determines the possibility of describing Kristeva's work as a polylogue. The term *polylogue*, so rich in connotations (is it a multiplication of the Platonic logos? of the Aristotelian logic? of the Lacanian signifier? of the Bakhtinian dialogue? or, to put it the other way round, is it a transposition of the Bakhtinian polyphonic novel into theory?), is introduced as the title to one of Kristeva's books. The very manner in which the term is unraveled hereafter is indicative. In the preface to her book, the polylogue is defined with theory as its starting point. It is presented as a multiplication of rationality, clearly relying on an interdisciplinary endeavor. It is described as a procedure that requires the positing, each time, of a unique subject, and appeals to the inimitable and the irretrievable. In this perspective, the polylogue is postulated as the stratification of logic in singular accounts, a stratification that results from the semanalytic invocation of the unnameable. It thus might be seen as a movement of theory toward the novel.

From within the book, however, from one of its essays, entitled "The Novel as a Polylogue," the term emerges in the redoubling of the quest of a female theoretician with the signifying practice of a male artist. A novel-as-text encounters an embodied subject of theory. The resulting clash enacts the polylogue no longer as a multiple splitting of logic, but as a shattering of the body in the rhythmic enunciation of a pain that severs the "self, the body, and each organ" (Kristeva 1980, p. 184). The agent of this pain is introduced as a musical ordering of language, as an ability to hold all the timbres of enunciation together, and, finally, as a reversal of the breaking up of genres, so that all the strings of this prodigious instrument that language is are played together and simultaneously (Kristeva 1980). What descends (from the conceptual heaven of theory) as a multiplication of logic, ascends (from within artistic practice) as the reunification of literary genres. The two movements collide in the precise jouissance of a body/text.

The result of this collision (of theory and artistic practice, of precision and jouissance, of semiotic and symbolic operations) is defined by Kristeva as nonsynthetic joining,[1] a concurrent nonsynthesis of logic and pain. Distinct but simultaneous. Separate but coextensive. Engaged in a multiple disjunctive dialogism. Sustained by an asymmetrically split heteronomous subject. It is important that we do not mistake the polylogue, the genus of a theory conscious of its narrative and semiotic dimensions, for a parable that exhausts the domain of the subject. As the genre mindful of the subject's hazards and rebirths, the polylogue is a space that Kristeva situates later on within the exemplary open-ended structures of analytic love. It can be entered (through curiosity or pain), and exited (through the effective cure). Hence it has an outside containing the possibilities of the subject's utter annihilation as well as its utopian health. The polylogue articulates the mean between annihilation and health, pointing toward utopia yet always returning to the problematic site that makes utopia necessary.

Within these boundaries, the polylogue sounds the registers partaking of the mother from the semanalytic exploration of the outer borders of the signifying venture of man (Kristeva 1980) that formulates new tasks for theory to the somatic shattering and jubilation. It is probably necessary to be a woman, Kristeva adds, aware as she is of the inanity of Being, in order to admit the subject of theory as a subject in infinite analysis, and to take up an exorbitant wager. The wager that will endow us, not with a resurrection but with multiple rebirths from the deluge of the drives, and that will teach us to tolerate multiple logics, speeches, and existences (Kristeva 1977). What gives meaning to the intellectual risks of the polylogic

---

1. Kristeva applies this description to the "paragrammatic" or "intertextual" reading of two simultaneous but distinct utterances (Kristeva 1969, p. 195), as well as to the "complementary opposition" (Kristeva 1984, p. 220) of the two different authorial personae in Lautréamont's writing.

project, ultimately, is the effective recognition of otherness as the formulation of a new basis for communication and togetherness.

Should we, then, read Kristeva's oeuvre as a polylogue?

FEMINIST CRITIQUES OF KRISTEVA'S MATERNAL FIGURE

The fact that Kristeva writes about motherhood drew a lot of attention in the feminist literature of the 1980s. In most cases this attention was critical and focused on two texts: "Motherhood According to Giovanni Bellini" (in Kristeva 1980), and "Stabat Mater" (in Kristeva 1986, 1987b). Kristeva, in spite of the shifts in the methodological paradigm that her work underwent throughout the years, is a meticulous and systematic thinker. The analysis of her texts out of their theoretical context was in itself a misfortune. The lack of attention to the work as a whole (as a body of work but also as a body of work related to other works, to an epistemological context, to a theoretical dialogical field) is one of the most common effects of abjectivity. Abjectivity oversteps the presumption that the language and the theoretical postulates of a thinker warrant the effort to be understood before being criticized. More recently, this type of attitude coalesced, in an infamous attack on Judith Butler, in Martha Nussbaum's (1999) performative demonstration that critique can in principle be implemented as a refusal of the effort to understand. All women should be able to understand immediately what a woman wrote. In the case of Nussbaum, the "all women" is dramatically represented as all those women who are hungry, illiterate, disenfranchised, beaten, raped all the way from America to India. Typically, the abjective reading destroys the specificity of its object by projecting it against the mass of all women (those who are raped, those who play basketball, those who were born elsewhere and to whom, alas, Nussbaum wants to export her help, and many, many others up to and including those who have the feminism that cares for all of them). Elaine Showalter, whose abjective essay on Woolf is discussed in Chapter 4, had a quicker way to name this background—she called it female experience and showed that Woolf did not fit. Against the background of all those real bodies and those real struggles, Nussbaum sums up Butler's theory in a manner that culminates in an invitation to thumb our noses. The transmutation of texts into punishable bodies is another typical feature of the abjective stance. In such instances, one should be always on the lookout for the paternal authority in the name of which all women are invoked to unite in order to massacre the one who dared be singular. Nussbaum takes care to stage the slaughter under the approving gaze of a whole host of male authorities, beginning with Socrates and not bypassing John Stuart Mill. With Showalter (1999), the paternal figure emerged recently in a statement that her title *A Literature of Their Own* did not refer to Woolf's famous title, *A Room of One's Own*, but to a quotation from John Stuart Mill. Later on, I will analyze this sacrificial rhetorical operation in greater detail in connection with the abjection of Woolf's "female aestheticism."

The critical responses to Kristeva that I want to discuss here were not exactly abjective but, nevertheless, there was a certain haste to discover the guilty woman behind the theory. Many of the various critiques converged in the belief that her theory had a disarticulating effect. There was little agreement, however, as to whom her theory disarticulated. According to one group of opinions, Kristeva's theory disarticulated the mother either by projecting the muteness of the infant on her, as Kaja Silverman (1988) believed, or by sacrificing her to the exigencies of theory: "The discourse of maternity gives birth to Kristevan poetics" (Jacobus 1986, p. 170). According to another group of opinions, represented by Domna Stanton (1986), by focusing on the dyad mother/male artist, Kristeva reinforced the prevalent privileging of male artists and disarticulated the woman artist. Yet another group of critics maintained that, by refusing to set up the semiotic no longer seen in a reductive light as an alternative to the symbolic and female libido as an alternative to the male one, Kristeva designates female homosexuality as a culturally unintelligible practice, inherently psychotic (Butler 1990).[2] And finally, it was argued that the disarticulation applied to woman in general: the chora was believed (Rose 1986) to smuggle directly its platonic reduction of the feminine to a container without any inherent relation to the generation of the offspring. Or rather, as a structural manifestation of the failure of Kristeva to transcend Lacan, the chora and the semiotic remained, according to Elizabeth Grosz (1989), beyond woman's grasp because of woman's asymbolia.

After Kelly Oliver's *Reading Kristeva* (1993) and the emergence, in the 1990s, of a Pacific Kristevan school (Lechte 1990, Lechte and Zournazi 1998, Smith 1996), it became clear that Kristeva's theory is not disarticu-

---

2. Judith Butler's later book *Bodies that Matter* (1993) seems to contain a reevaluation of Kristeva. Butler's subsequent development (1997) of the concept of the abject transposes this term into a totally different set of theoretical preoccupations.

lating anybody. With this realization, the debate somehow petered out. This happened precisely at the time when the carefully prepared theoretical premises for the conceptualization of the feminine and the maternal took Kristeva to her most systematic explorations (Kristeva 1996, 2000a, 2002a). How are we to relate Kristeva's views of female asymbolia, which she does hold, to her belief that perhaps a woman is necessary to take up the wager of carrying the rational project to the outer borders of the signifying venture of men? How can her ideas of woman as asymbolic singularity be reconciled with the persistent Kristevan theme of woman's eternal exile, where exile is a vantage point for a polylogic rebirth of meaning? Kristeva has come up with some formidable answers to these questions.

ASYMBOLIA

"Fear of the archaic mother turns out to be essentially fear of her generative power. It is this power, a dreaded one, that patrilineal filiation has the burden of subduing" (Kristeva 1982, p. 77). "Phallic power, in the sense of a symbolic power that thwarts the traps of penial performance, would in short begin with an appropriation of archaic maternal power" (Kristeva 1987b, p. 75). "Phallic idealization is built upon the pedestal of a putting-to-death of the feminine body" (p. 357).

The murder of the feminine body and its evacuation from the phallic order founds woman's asymbolia. Asymbolia is the condition of woman with regard to a symbolic that functions through the exclusion of the feminine. According to Kristeva's account in the untranslated sections of *The Revolution in Poetic Language*, this condition is effected through a complicity between the state and mystery. Such a complicity guarantees the disjunction between production and reproduction and occludes genitality. In this way, the symbolic may afford to remain ignorant of sexual difference, and mystery may practice it under the condition that it does not know it.

The emphasis on mystery as the reverse, hidden side of the law displaces the emphasis of Lévi-Strauss's approach that tends to neglect heterogeneity, or to treat it as a depository of laws. According to Kristeva, Lévi-Strauss's anthropological vision brackets the mother–child relationship. Her study of mystery extends her critique of the bracketing that sustains Lévi-Strauss's structures. As the unspoken double of the social code, mystery creates an alternative economy. It encloses the residues of a symbolic that, in Lévi-Strauss's account, treats women as objects of exchange.

Yet as the double of the symbolic, as the representation of heterogeneity for the symbolic, mystery also makes the efficiency of the code impeccable. Mystery submits heterogeneity to the exigencies of the law (this submission corresponds to the phallicization of the mother) and arrests the possibilities for structural change.

Within this arrangement, the feminine harbors the mystery and has no outlet into the symbolic. The eternal feminist movement of the suffragettes is in search of understanding woman's spastic force, which is presented as castration by the phallic culture. This force cannot find its proper representation and cannot be absorbed by the paranoid logic of the phratry that is offered to it. Two paths are open to woman: to find her specificity in a kind of asymbolic singularity, or to live in disguise, pretending that she observes the law that neither sees, nor signifies her (Kristeva 1977).

In woman's writing, language seems to be seen from a foreign land, Kristeva states in a much debated passage. Is it seen from the point of view of an asymbolic, spastic body? In a phrase that revives the drama of Andersen's "Little Mermaid," who dreams of the foreign land, the drama, that is, of a longing that has no tongue and that finds its expression in the piercing pain of separation (a separation from the sea-sisters and a separation of the body for swimming into a body for walking), Kristeva speaks of women as "visionaries, dancers who suffer as they speak" (Kristeva 1981, p. 166).

The disturbing poignancy of the passage does not come so much from its "Little Mermaid" pathos but rather from its example: Virginia Woolf, a writer who seems to have been as close to becoming the voice of the Zeitgeist as a woman has ever been able to, and who has been persistently dislocated from that position. Did this dislocation come about because of asymbolia? Because Woolf as Kristeva puts it "does not dissect language as Joyce does" (Kristeva 1981, p. 166)?

POETRY, IRONY, REBELLION

In her recent work, Kristeva elaborates this situation of women through the careful spelling out of a biphasic Oedipus and an "other libido." The girl gains access to the phallic order while bearing the unconscious traces of Oedipus One—of the polymorphous sensory fusion with the mother, which leaves on her the indelible imprint of an endogenous homosexuality. It should be noted that the preoedipal mother of Kristeva's early work has been transformed into an Oedipus One mother, and the objectless female quasi-libido (I will return to this) has become an "other libido." The girls succeed in accessing the phallic order—which is erected on the fundament of the invisible Minoan-Mycenaean continent—in the modality of "as if," of a constitutive exclusion that amounts to radical foreignness, and of irreparable solitude. This foreignness and this solitude, however, may serve as the basis for a rebellion and for a critical distancing that Hegel described as the "eternal irony of the community" (Kristeva 2002a, pp. 554–555).

It is worth keeping in mind the fact, therefore, that Woolf's position, as described by Kristeva, exemplifies not only the feminine position per se but also the position that allows the "revolution in poetic language," the making and unmaking of the subject and its signs. Already in her first book in French—with the exotic title Σημειωτικὴ—Kristeva insists on the necessity for us to be or to become "strangers to language" in order to make it work (Kristeva 1969, p. 9). We have to stop understanding it and look at it from the position of a radical incomprehension, we have to become language's foreigners. We have to situate ourselves in the feminine.

This strangeness to language does entail the forlornness of the melancholic who is fused with the maternal Thing because of an unaccomplished separation from the mother. Asymbolia is the insufficiently lost maternal continent, the invisible center of gravity, the hidden image of Narcissus, whose silent call threatens with dissolution. But, on the other hand, without an ear for that silence and without the estrangement from language that prods the melancholic on a quest for the totally new word, there can be no psychic life or imagination. As Kristeva argues in *Strangers to Ourselves* (1991), there can be no basis for understanding and cooperation, no hope for the paradoxical universality demanded by a world without boundaries. Woman's asymbolia, the feminine, Woolf's speaking with the difficulty of a visionary and a dancer, with the painful force of a spastic body, offers the horizon for a new universality that respects the unique and the singular.

In all cases the estrangement (*ostranenie*) of asymbolia is the proper beginning for the singing work of language. Kristeva's theoretical preoccupation with what is excluded, with the outside of discourse, a preoccupation that overlaps with the topology of the lost mother, specifies her perspective on asymbolia. Insofar as she is asymbolic, woman inhabits that place where unique incommunicable meanings hold sway. Wavering between masquerade (femininity) and asymbolic singularity (the feminine), she encompasses the modern choice between a theatrical, ludic subjectivity (the *je* of *jeu*) and a problematic, unexchangeable uniqueness.

It is true that the valorization of unique reports undermines the importance of communication and exchange. In Kristeva's early writing, the productivity of language is emphatically set against its communicative aspect. The polylogue promises the generality of a logic and, in the long run, the hope for a community of strangers. And yet, the emphasis is on marking the existence of a life rather than on making the life communicable. Only in infinity will the lovers meet; the transferential relationship, this modern love story, is not an encounter, not an attainment of the other. It is a technique for opening the psychic space toward a vibrant balancing upon the razor's edge of a world where certainties, final answers, and dogmas are no longer possible. Writing is a creative opening on this side that comes from a wandering on the far side, from a secret concern with a hidden face, a silent sister. The possibility for a subtilization of the superego comes from the silence and the concealment, from the obscure continent of the feminine. The multiplication of rationality is achieved through the movement toward the unnameable (toward primary repression, the unknown of mystery, genitality, the mother). Such is the polylogic wager offered to asymbolic singularity.

NOT THIS

How can theory posit an object that is beyond its limits? How can it make an object out of that which departs from meaning? By positing itself as nonuniversal, runs one of Kristeva's answers,

> that is, by presupposing that a questionable subject-in-process exists in an economy of discourse other than that of thetic consciousness. And this requires that subjects of the theory must be themselves subjects in infinite analysis. [Kristeva 1980, p. 146]

This confrontation between the subject of theory and the subject of a heterogeneous economy enacts the sliding of the theoretical signifier, a technique that sets off the nonuniversality of theoretical discourses. This technique is most clearly exemplified in the method of *The Revolution in Poetic Language*, which consecutively proceeds through general theories of meaning, theories of language, and theories of the subject in order to demonstrate their indispensability and inadequacy for describing the object of Kristeva's inquiry. The method has been defined as montage, but is more precisely described as a stratification of the theoretical discourse in a manner that resists one-dimensional filiations and loyalties, and that approaches its object via a number of distinct routes. This multigenealogy continues to show up in Kristeva's subsequent writing. The privileged theoretical position of psychoanalysis in it seems to derive ultimately from a gesture that points outside theory, toward an understanding of truth as the capacity for renovation and rebirth.

The stratification of theoretical discourse is one way to question the foundations of universality. Another way is provided by the subject of a heterogeneous economy, which has numerous topoi as well. In her early work Kristeva posits the necessity for a nonreductive typology of semiotic practices. Later on this necessity is exemplified by an open series of inquiries into a variety of subjective positions that allow glimpses of the unspeakable: inquiries into diverse modalities of access to the symbolic function. A double star of a sort is thus formed in which an emptiness or irrevocable silence is accosted through the rays of various theoretical concepts (Heraclitus's matter that is always already split, Plato's chora, Hegel's negativity, Freud's death drive, etc.). This advance from the point of view of the theoretical subject, with all the difficulties that its position imposes on pursuits of this kind, is then mediated through a second star of various destabilized, precarious subjects within a field edged by poetry and madness: the abject in *Powers of Horror*, the melancholic in *Black Sun*, the sequence of forlorn or ecstatic lovers in *Tales of Love*, and, most recently, the female geniuses in the Arendt–Klein–Colette trilogy. The redoubling of the subject, characteristic of Kristeva's work, is thus part of her project. Through this redoubling of the theoretical subject with the various subjects of a heterogeneous economy, the concept achieved through the difficult reasoning of the philosophers becomes the abject, the thing, the lost territory, the *fons amoris*, ecstasy, jouissance. The feminine. The vide central. Not this. For we cannot enunciate this constitutive absence from which our horror and bliss spring; what we can do is, by invoking the abyss, by wandering at the limits of the thinkable, subtilize the superego and our concepts of rationality.

THE EPISTEMOLOGICAL SPACE

The redoubling of the subject of Kristeva's stratified theoretical discourse marks a shift in the theoretical focus from the problem of the operations of the I to the problem of the process that produces this I. What we are asking is: How did this consciousness manage to posit itself? Our concern, therefore, is not the operating and producing consciousness, but rather the producible consciousness (Kristeva 1984).[3] In her early work, referring to Peirce's classification of science, Kristeva suggests a definition of semiotics as the theory that explores the time (chronotheory) and the topography (topotheory) of the signifying act (Kristeva 1969). Hence one of the moves that inaugurate her project concerns a topotheoretical operation: the recognition of the epistemological space as split into two irreconcilable types of thought where "the one is articulated only through its ignorance of the other: representation and its production, the ratiocination of objects and the dialectic of their process (of their becoming)" (Kristeva 1977, p. 231).

This recognition of the epistemological space as split, always open, and never saturated results from the realization that the production of the sign and of the subject cannot be given within the homogeneous sphere of concepts and ideas. Such a study requires another type of logic and a heterogeneous economy: an epistemological space observable only through some discordance in the symbolic function. The various indications of such a discordance and the knowledge about the producible consciousness that they provide are at the center of Kristeva's theoretical interest. From the examination of the permanently stabilized and destabilized interaction of the semiotic and the symbolic to the elaboration of the various modes of the subject's leap into the realm of signs, Kristeva's consistent aim is to demonstrate the dynamic character of the relationship between the symbolic and the heterogeneous economy that works it. It is, perhaps, worth repeating at this point that the question, for Kristeva, is not how consciousness in general came into being, but rather how *this* consciousness came into being. Consciousness is regarded as a historically and geographically circumscribed problem. One of Kristeva's Marxian projects, as manifested in *La Traversée des Signes*, is to find out whether different modes of production are bound up with different types of subject-formations and signifying practices. The project is left aside in her later work in a simultaneous movement away from the Marxian and the non-Occidental problematic and toward an intensification of her focus on the micrology of the signifying process. Nevertheless, this unfinished project indicates that, for Kristeva, there are culturally and historically specific aspects to the signifying practice and to the making and

---

3. The translation in the main text is confusing: Kristeva does not ask "what the 'I' produces" (1984; p. 36) but what produces the "I" (1974, p. 35).

unmaking of the subject. The variability of the law is bound up with a variable configuration of the mystery. The discordance that Kristeva proposes to study, although offering a vertiginous glimpse of infinite splitting, provides a message that is contingent on the symbolic disrupted by it. Music is Kristeva's case of pure semiosis but music is also one of the most obvious examples of the culturally specific shackling of negativity. The study of the revolution in poetic language is framed by developments pertaining to French prosody. The examination of motherhood is inseparable from the forms that Western art and religion have bestowed on it. The loss of psychic space diagnosed in *Tales of Love* is a loss for the no longer tenable Occidental Christian soul with its Greek and Judaic lineage. And so on. Hence, in spite of Kristeva's insistence on the fake, the illusory, and the ludic, one should not lose sight of the very concrete exigencies that summon them. "To every ego its object, to every superego its abject" (Kristeva 1982, p. 2). But also, to every symbolic its traversée—its specific subversion.

TIME: THE αἰὼν

The disruptive space of the sign's and the subject's production necessitates a chronotheoretical approach: the elaboration of logical and chronological priorities, that is, the linearization of a synchronic functioning. It thus involves a specific mode of temporality, which Kristeva (1980) discusses in *Place Names* in terms of the emergence of the child in Freud's theory. The child emerges as the residue of the subtraction of guilt from mastery. This residue of the metamorphosis of the child into a parent is a telescoping of parent and child that presents us with a child always already older, inscribed by "a narrative 'texture,' that is, a texture of language and phantasm" (Kristeva 1980, p. 276). Dictated by adult memory and articulated by the adult analyst, the child whose triangulated familial problematic serves to explain the production of the speaking subject, is inescapably that speaking subject's product: the speaking subject cannot be dealt with through a child at zero degree of symbolism or at the level of the drive. Hence any questions of priority and precedence have to be very carefully framed: the child or, for that matter, the semiotic chora of which such questions are often asked may be logically and chronologically prior to the adult (the symbolic), yet we have them always as an epistemological corollary.

This analytic circularity joining cause and effect is designated by Kristeva as an *aion* on the basis of Heraclitus's 52d fragment: αἰὼν παῖς ἐστι παίζων πεσσεύων παιδὸς ἡ βασιληίη (Robinson 1987). Or, in G. S. Kirk's (1954) translation, "Aion is a child at play, playing draughts; the kingship is a child's" (p. xiii). As the translation itself suggests, Kristeva's use of *aion* as a designation of circularity draws us into another circularity. The Heraclitean *aion* presents a classical hermeneutical problem: its meaning is undecidable within the context of this "most puzzling of Heraclitus's statements" (Robinson 1987, p. 116). Kirk limits the scope of options by including the fragment among the anthropocentric rather than the cosmic fragments: he makes a choice in favor of *aion* as lifetime rather than time in general. The child playing is not a cosmic child of some kind with a kingship over all things absolutely. Rather, it is a figure referring to the working out of individual destiny. The decision is based on Kirk's interpretation of the rest of Heraclitus's fragments and depends on the uncertainties of this interpretation: one might hold the opposite view, as Robinson does. For once, therefore, we do not have to refer to Heidegger's penchant for speculative translation when he affirms that what is named in *aion* resists precisely the distinction that Kirk and Robinson make from two opposing perspectives. The *aion*, according to Heidegger (1961), "means the whole of the world, but also time, and, related by time to our 'life', it means the course of life itself" (p. 77).

So is the *aion* eternity, time in general, lifetime, all this, or something altogether different? In the face of this uncertainty, what we are left with is the child playing. Whether the emphasis is on the game's rules, or on the arbitrariness of the rules; whether the child's royal power refers to cruel randomness and youthful irresponsibility (which is unlikely in view of the elevated status that Heraclitus bestows on children), or to some sort of Schiller-Kleistean antigravitational grace, is again indeterminate. In one case at least, however, the French translators, Bollack and Wismann, have decided to avoid the redundancy of the usual translations of Heraclitus's phrase (a child at play, playing) and render the first playing (παίζων) through a mobilization of the etymological meaning that relates it to child (παῖς): thus παίζων becomes making a child, engendering, giving birth. Do we have to point out that this etymological reinterpretation amounts to a backward translation into Greek of the French *enfanter*, which has precisely the meanings that the translators ascribe to παίζων? Do we have to add that the Greek phrase does not repeat the word for play and hence, perhaps, does not require measures for avoiding a redundancy that is far less obvious in it than in its translations? And do we have to complain that the translators ignore the kind of game that the child is playing (draughts), thus giving up its possible (but very problematic) implications? What matters for the time being is the *aion* that engenders, playing, the meaning of fragment 52. It is Bollack and Wismann's translation that Kristeva refers to, and for good reasons, as we shall see.

What we read now is, *"La vie est bien un enfant qui enfante, qui joue"* (Bollack 1972, p. 182). In a superb final touch, the English translators, Gora, Jardine, and Roudiez, render Bollack and Wismann's *enfant* as newborn. The αἰών (to go back to Kristeva's use of the term in the silent Greek alphabet) thus becomes "a newborn who bears, who plays" (Kristeva 1980, p. 292, n. 9). Wonderful! For migrating from language to language, circulating through the *aion* of polyglottic engendering, what we have witnessed being born is the child of Kristeva's theory. Not the always already older child of the Freudian subtraction of guilt from mastery. In a truly *aionic* manner, fragment 52 as a newborn who bears, who plays, gives birth to/is born from the Kristevan child. It incorporates (1) Kristeva's emphasis on the site sustaining the sign's and the subject's making and unmaking; (2) Kristeva's problematization of birth as giving birth to the other, self-birth, and rebirth; and (3) Kristeva's theoretical and, we might say, theatrical preoccupation with play and the drama of the I (the *je* of *jeu*) as masquerade, polyglottism, and work-in-progress. The infinite analysis (of the subject of theory) that Kristeva's polylogue demands can now be described as the time space, the *aion*, of giving birth to the child that bears its genetrix in a ludic renovation of meaning. The work/play of rebirth: to a child belongs dominion.

FEMALE LIBIDO

Female libido is a Kristevan term that evolves out of Winnicott and Klein, that is subtended (like most things in Kristeva) by the death drive, and that designates a specific type of correlation between drives and the symbolic. Like Freud's male libido, which is common to men and women and informs any erotic relationship, the female libido is not applicable to only certain groups of people. It is an amorous space approachable from any gender position. Male libido and female libido pertain to a typology of loves and not to a typology of bodies. In her recent work Kristeva accentuates that female libido is an other libido (by dividing the Oedipus phase into Oedipus One and Oedipus Two she evades the gendering of the Oedipal phase without foreclosing the possibility for conceptualizing the feminine beyond gender identities). Her claim is that the powers and applications of the other libido are mobilized by the metaphoric leap of *Einfühlung*,[4] rather than the metonymic flight of desire; and that it is anchored in the cavernous receptivity of Oedipus One (Kristeva 2002a).

If the Freudian child springs from the death of the father's father 'the father is dead, long live the father that I am' and if this child, born into the world with "compound drives, erogenous zones, and even genital desires" (Kristeva 1980, p. 275), acquires its form within the oedipal triangle, the Kristevan infant emerges in the recovery of the body of the mother's mother through the act of giving birth. This gloss on the Freudian equation of the child to a penis-substitute (since giving birth gives an access for the daughter to the body of her mother) situates the newborn in an unusual triangle. The other two parties in this triangle are the mother and her mother, a precarious triangle formed by the amplification of the mother–child dyad. The female libido, therefore, is the space or no-space in which a mother attains the infinite body of her death-proof mother. The mother lives, long live the mother that I am. It is in this atopia, traced by Kristeva with reference to Winnicott's potential space, that the earliest dramas of the future speaking being take place.

This triangle, which in Kristeva's early work is posited as objectless but which she now sees in Kleinian terms as already having an object, is inscribed within the site of the smallest and most uncertain of differences. The analysis through which the infant both reunites and precludes the symbiotic fusion of the mother and her mother wields enormous powers but also poses great risks. For if, on the one hand, this is the "not yet a place" in which woman adjoins her first love object that had to be replaced through the oedipal exigencies, the reunion has the aspect of a total erotization that ushers in mystic and ecstatic merging. In its measureless radiance, the female libido is seen by Kristeva as the *fons amoris* behind the histories of our loves (rather than sexuality), the narcissistic support that creates our inner space, the mysterious raison d'être of the stability of the couple, and, most recently, the matrix for the social link per se. However, insofar as this triangulation of minimal differences is marked by instability and a tendency of its positions to merge or replace each other, in other

---

4. This Freudian term is rendered in English and French as "identification." Its prehistory in nineteenth-century hermeneutics implies a mystic emotional fusion, or, as Kristeva's gloss has it, "the assimilation of other people's feelings" (Kristeva 1987b, p. 24).

words insofar as the minimal differences are maintained only with the greatest difficulty—this place-to-come has the aspect of a struggle between a woman and another, her mother, in which the infant becomes ensnared as a pawn rather than an analyst. For the mother, the birth of the child is a reversed reactivation, but reversal does not mean much in this situation—of the symbiosis with her mother through which she had to struggle. The difficulty that a woman has in separating from the maternal Thing is thus due not only to her being the same. It is due also to the exigency that reproduces the fusion and the trial of separation. As such, the atopia of female libido is the place of horror and abjection.

A threat to identity, in both cases. The loss of the mother is thus not only inevitable but also necessary (for the mother herself). The unaccomplished separation from the mother is seen by Kristeva as a frequent phenomenon among women: blocking the emergence of one's proper body, the mother arrested within is held accountable for frigidity ("I am full I cannot be entered"), for the resistance to pleasure ("How can I enjoy if I have to lose my mother?"), as well as for the inhibition of action and the underrating of language. The removal of this hindrance does not yet answer the problems with the symbolic itself ("I am to leave my mother in order to go where?"), nor does it promise the advent of the man who can allow, without falling apart, the realization that he has been enjoyed by a woman (has been used as an object of pleasure rather than as symbolic authority). Even so, Kristeva's analysis of female libido deserves closer scrutiny for, besides disclosing the ways in which culture is worked by the love originating with the mother–child dyad, it may also provide a clue to some baffling questions. Namely, if the demand for psychic parturition turns the mother that bears into a devouring mother, how does the devouring mother become the one that is devoured? And if it is the mother who gets devoured and lost, how is it, for a woman, that the lost mother turns into fatherlessness (asymbolia)?

Let us go back to the emergence of the Freudian and the Kristevan child. The Freudian child surfaces from the subtraction of guilt from mastery in the settling of accounts between a father and his dead father. The father is purged through the locating of guilt in the always older and seducing child. He replaces the dead father. He occupies the space of a clearing that keeps the father and his father distinct, diachronic, and at a safe distance from the liabilities of seduction. The infant, however, insists on a libidinal-signifying organization different from that of the adult (what Kristeva has designated as the semiotic). It is born on the precarious boundary between the mother and the body of her mother. It thus restores a phantasmatic presence, a phantasmatic fusion barely ever overcome. "A woman is her mother," as Anne Sexton put it. Or, as it has been persistently repeated, if the father is "an unreality set apart, who, from the beginning, is a being of language" (Ricoeur 1970, p. 542) and a figure of absence; if it is through absence and separation that the symbolic functions, the mother is the one always present.

Not a metaphysics but a physics of presence. A phantasmatic physics, of course. Kristeva's preoccupation is to unravel the routes of this phantasm and to insist both on its creative potential and on the irrevocable absence and loss that it screens. Through this absence, the mother becomes present. For, if an always-thereness, an unbroken physical presence devours the mother through a refusal to distinguish between the mother and her mother, it is the confrontation with the mother's absence and with the void that her loss entails that gives her back as a maternal gesture extended across language.

REDUPLICATION

The zone demarcated by the female libido has, according to Kristeva, its proper language: reduplication. Reduplication is a "jammed repetition" (Kristeva 1989, p. 246). Unlike repetition, reduplication is devoid of duration, it is outside of time. Its medium is the false space created by the play of mirrors and the reverberations of echoes, by the hypnotic passion that sees only doubles. It is the fathomless exploration, the *mise en abîme* of the same; the uncovering of the same secret depths that threaten to engulf it.

Kristeva elaborates her ideas of reduplication through a study of Marguerite Duras's work. While the pages dedicated to Duras are among Kristeva's most powerful and, we might say, hypnotic achievements, they also occupy a curious place within the analysis of melancholy, of the unaccomplished separation from the maternal Thing, that is carried out in *Black Sun*. Duras's writing, indifferent to the modernist concerns with the music of speech or with the dismantling of narrative logic, is described as offering an "aesthetics of awkwardness and a literature without catharsis" (Kristeva 1989, p. 225). Her sentences are seen as lacking acoustic charm and her books are perceived as dangerous for the oversensitive reader who might give in to their spell and remain arrested by the affliction that they recognize but also propagate; these books do not offer the consolations of rhetoric, the purging cure of artifice, or the festive animation that even everyday speech possesses. Duras's use of language reveals an underrating of language, an awareness of its powerlessness. Language thus almost gives way; it is pushed aside for a confrontation with nothingness and the silence of horror. Devoid of catharsis, of purification, or forgiveness, Duras's writing remains "on the near side of any warping of meaning, confining itself to baring the malady" (Kristeva 1989, p. 229).

A literature without literariness, an art without artifice, a horror without sublimity? But also a historicity outside of time, a politics outside of the public realm: in the spectrum of private suffering. It is true that all portraits of melancholy artists in *Black Sun* share a transhistoric quality that pertains to the timeless and atopical space of unaccomplished separation from the mother. It is also true that in all these cases the private suffering of the artist is interwoven with a historical crisis that is hence uncovered: Holbein and the crisis of the Christian subject during the Reformation, Nerval and the crisis of values in the nineteenth century, Dostoevsky and the pending Russian revolution, and Duras and the apocalyptic dimension of the twentieth century. In all these cases, however, with the exception of Duras, the artists also offer a solution: Holbein creates beauty out of deadness, Nerval extracts an Orphic victory out of madness, and Dostoevsky evolves forgiveness out of the destructive allures of suicide and terrorism. Duras is the one who offers nothing but a stark confrontation with distress and pain. Instead of a solution, Duras presents "a world of unsettling, infectious ill-being" (Kristeva 1989, p. 258). The work of Holbein, Nerval, and Dostoevsky is triggered by a timeless private suffering but it offers its solution to an epoch; the affliction in Duras's fiction is triggered and increased by the insanity of the contemporary world but it nevertheless "proves to be essential and transhistorical" (Kristeva 1989, p. 258). Outside of time.

There is a paradox involved in this situation. It is precisely Duras's ahistorical quality that makes her historically representative for her epoch, an epoch rendered speechless by apocalyptic suffering; it is the absorption of politics by the personal that epitomizes her contemporary political choice; and it is out of Duras's resistance to meaning that Kristeva weaves the meaning of her world. The paradox itself, however, cannot conceal another movement in which Duras's writing is held captive. For in its ahistoricity and awkward a-literariness, in its closeness to clinical discourse without the cure, Duras's work of reduplication joins and enhances the narratives of Kristeva's own female patients and thus speaks the very timeless and atopical realm that Kristeva's study approaches: the realm of female libido, of the passion for the mother, of the murderous-and-suicidal drive for totality and fusion.

Are we offered, then, a theoretical variant of reduplication, of the hypnotic gaze? Does Duras become encrypted in the crypt that Kristeva's analysis delineates? Kristeva's artists, male or female, function more often than not as the doubles of her theoretical endeavor; the case with Duras, stripped of historical or aesthetic dimensions in order to reveal the very source of redoubling, of enthralled hatred and spellbinding passion, seems to be especially striking. Is it because "as an echo to death-bearing symbiosis with the mothers, passion between two women represents one of the most intense images of doubling" (Kristeva 1989, p. 250)?

INTERSEXUALITY

Kristeva's recent trilogy on Arendt, Klein, and Colette is a massive vindication of singularity as the ethos of her own theoretical position. Even before she turned to the female genius, however, she was preoccupied with the creative potential of the feminine. The male artists that she studied throughout the years, from Lautréamont to Proust, share a number of characteristics that make them strangely similar. They all are obsessed with the great maternal passion and many of them adopt their mother's (grandmother's, in Céline's case) name or esoterically play with it as in Lautréamont's phonetic and graphic transpositions (Kristeva 1974). For them, in one way or another, the signifying practice is a happily accomplished incest, opening up an excess of meaning as in the chromatic translucency of Bellini's painting or the stellar laughter of Dante's *Paradiso*. But it may also unfold the horror of collapsing boundaries and thus drive into a creativity accomplished as incessant flight. The artistic practice studied by Kristeva thus amounts to the appropriation—mysterious or violent, fetishist or psychotic of this *reverse* side, the support and source of power, that is the mother's strength and jouissance (Kristeva 1974). Hence Kristeva's male artists tend to usurp the feminine role. They find their double in a sister-figure that duplicates their own experience of what is exterior to the symbolic, and their problematic invocation to the outside of meaning.

A curious dynamic is thus formed. The male artists mirrored by their silent sisters become brothers mirroring Kristeva's theoretical endeavor. The couple, artist and silent sister, is reproduced as theoretician and brother artist in an incestuous embrace that mixes body and thought in one and the same trace (Kristeva 1977). It gives birth to its strange offspring, a presence in meaning as that meaning's outside. Kristeva's protagonists are *aionic* children who, playing, engender the theoretical subject who generates them in search of matters of her own concern.

LUDIC DISCIPLINE

The contrary movement reverses the quest of the theoretician and draws a trajectory from the limits of the thinkable, from the site of primary repression, to the register of the symbolic. It can be achieved through a shortcut that Kristeva terms "primary identification." Primary identification effects a direct transfer to an ideal other, to a unifying object that serves as a constitutive metaphor of the subject. Insofar as this identification amounts to the incorporation of a scheme, a model, of the very possibility for language, for distinction and differentiation, it is accomplished as fusion, communion, unification. It is thus an instantaneous translation—but involving a transposition into a heterogeneous register—of the female libido into love, Agape.

This archaic pole of idealization is a father–mother conglomerate, and combines the attributes of both parents. It is developed by Kristeva out of Freud's "father of individual prehistory," and out of Klein's conception of projective identification and the gratitude directed at the maternal object in its totality. Kristeva names this instance "imaginary father." As a heterogeneous translation, as a transposition that metaphorically relays the subject via an immediate leap to the place of the mother's desire, this idealizing movement originates in the most archaic of settings. Transforming the lost mother into an imaginary father, it can be regarded as the *Urform* of intertextuality. Is the role of the imaginary father, in a manner similar to the phallic mother's role as the uncompromising support of the relentless paternal Law, to support a symbolic less severe, more caring, tolerant, polylogic: maternal? "We are dealing with a function that guarantees the subject's entry into a modality, a fragile one to be sure, of the ulterior, unavoidable oedipal destiny, but one that can also be playful and sublimational" (Kristeva 1987b, p. 46). A function that, insofar as it carnivalizes the oedipal necessities, ensures the unfolding of the multiple speeches and existences that the polylogue demands. A function that turns discipline into play. A subtilization of the superego.

EROS AND NARCISSUS

Two ludic destinies are opened by this discipline. The first one is situated under the sign of Eros, of the male libido. Driven by the phantom of an ideal ego, it is inflated through the narcissistic absorption of the mother. It acquires its impetus from the developments of the oedipal stage. Fascinated by the visual, specular double of the phantasm of a primeval condition, it pursues, from one object to the next, the trajectory of a centrifugal and metonymic quest for an image that is never adequate, never the true one. Its outward thrust whose turbulent sublimational dialectic is first problematized by Plato and whose interminable sliding over the fugitive object of desire is perused by Lacan, finds its knowledgeable epitome in Don Juan's skepticism and in the principle of the seducer. Ludic and empty, unessential,the incessant flight of the seducer unfolds through a multiplication of spaces and through the shattering of identity into masks. The Mallarméan "Nothing will have taken place, but the place" runs like a refrain throughout Kristeva's work. It recapitulates this movement that offers to the modern soul its utopia of two plus two makes four: a polytopia sustained by mathematics and laughter.

The second movement is situated by Kristeva under the sign of Narcissus, the unheroic youth who died for the love of his image looking at him from the *vide* of the lost maternal space. Centripetal rather than centrifugal, unfolding through a metaphorical and heterogeneous leap rather than through metonymical sliding, amorous rather than desiring, verbal and musical rather than specular, the narcissistic operation takes us toward the scene of primary identification.

"What is the object for? It serves to give sexual existence to anguish. . . . The object of Narcissus is psychic space; it is representation itself, fantasy" (Kristeva 1987b, p. 116). It is Narcissus's tragic mistake to remain unaware of this truth of the objectlessness of his love. At the crisis of Antiquity, Plotinus corrects the mistake by reversing Narcissus's love away from the image and toward its source; he thus effects a synthesis between the platonic search for ideal beauty and the autoeroticism of one's proper image. Through an idealizing process that is incorporating rather than sublimating, neoplatonism interiorizes the platonic quest: beauty is incarnated in the inner space creating the light of Occidental internality, of the Occidental soul.

It is Kristeva's point that we should revisit the fragile and archaic settings of the Narcissus scene. Not in order to repeat the neoplatonic movement toward the luminous closure of a self-love, no longer possible, but in order to gaze once again at the image, knowledgeably this time, and with a full awareness of its fakeness and its irreality. It is with a view to our lucidity as the creators of images and to our knowledgeable love for our own creations that Kristeva evokes, from the Narcissus settings, the figure of the imaginary father. The narcissistic movement toward the imaginary father offers a ludic opening of our destiny. It repeats the neoplatonic incorporation of the erotic quest, but not its closure. A constellation is thus added to the unfurling of empty spaces; the seducer is internalized into a creator in love with her creations. This gift, the love of our irreal creations, a maternal love par excellence, as any reader who ever sympathized with Mary Shelley's monster knows, may be needed by a future humanity more than we can imagine today.

QUANTA, PROTOZOA, AND EXTRATERRESTRIALS

The subtilization of the superego, as problematized by Kristeva via her *aionic* explorations, relies, therefore, on (1) an attentiveness to the heterogeneity of drives and to their archaic hold on the maternal continent; (2) an explication of the permanent process of stabilization-destabilization in which the symbolic and the semiotic are implicated; (3) an insistence on the multiplicity of modalities of access to the symbolic function; and (4) an emphasis on the feminine as the modality of rebellion and renewal. It is derivable ultimately from the elaboration of a position of symbolicity, a position that arises from primary identification, which launches us immediately into the place of the maternal desire, and which makes possible the emergence of the imaginary father as the promise of a ludic entry into the oedipal exigencies. This is the promise of a polylogic unfolding of language, and of a life quivering on the edge of permanent undecideability.

Does, consequently, the quest for the mother yield a . . . father? "A strange father it must be," writes Kristeva in connection with Freud's father of individual prehistory that she elaborates into her own concept of the imaginary father. For this father is, of course, also the mother. But then a strange mother! For this mother-and-father belongs to a modality that is ignorant of gender and, ultimately, it is pointless to ask "who might be the object of primary identification, daddy or mummy" (Kristeva 1987b, p. 28). This uncertainty, requiring as it does its concrete ramifications, can nevertheless be expanded beyond the stage of primary identification. It is true that phallic idealization begins with "the putting to death of the feminine body" and with the "appropriation of female generative power—a dreaded power; that paternal law emerges as a substitute for and an occultation of the crucial importance of the mother and of the maternal jouissance" (Kristeva 1974, p. 457). And yet it is also a truth that "the phallus is the mother" (Kristeva 1980, p. 191), and that maternal power replaces and veils the murdered father (Kristeva 1974). The occluded generative power as the phallus, as the Name of the father, as the phallic mother, and as the dead father inscribes a quantum layer in the signifying process—a layer of uncertainty and complementarity that makes the simultaneous clarity of all parameters impossible, but that also manifests their alliance. At any moment in the advent of the speaking being or in the functioning of the city, the maternal and the paternal are always already substitutes for one another, symbols of one another, present and absent, dead and vibrant with power.

If there is a *texture* of a sorts that might be seen as underlying this fundamental uncertainty, it is a texture of nothingness: the death drive. Kristeva asserts that language, already as a semiotic chora but above all as a symbolic system, is at the service of the death drive (Kristeva 1984). And even more strongly, "language is the terrain of deathwork" (Kristeva 1983, p. 38). Language is the master that diverts and confines the death drive, yet only through the paradox that makes death produce both life and signification.

Through the death drive's reiteration. Kristeva's postulate points toward Freud's definition of the drive as inherent inertia and as the gravitating of life toward the inorganic state that it has been forced to abandon. In Freud, this definition in terms of mechanics finds its biological example in the propagation through scission that preceded sexual reproduction: a myth inviting us back to the primeval suicidal impulse of the protozoan whose splitting initiated the perpetuation of its species and the multiplication of cells that made higher forms of life possible. Later developments have added dramatically to this picture by revealing that the splitting is, indeed, a reproduction of the memory of the cell; that the splitting copies the writing of the genetic code through the redoublings and reversals of the double helix. The separation, the abyss that opens in the slit, is thus both reproductive and signifying; it is this signifying aspect that Kristeva adds to Freud's biological myth. Kristeva's concept of language as ultimately the work of death thus introduces the problem of signification within the most primal settings; there is, she insists, an archaic inscription of the third party at the early stage that Melanie Klein, the audacious theoretician of the death drive, elaborates. Hence, for Kristeva, signification itself can be thought of as an echo of the processes of separation in biochemistry; the death drive, regarded by Freud as silent and discernible only in instinctual disorders, is described by Kristeva as "that which speaks" (Kristeva 1974, p. 611) through incision and repetition. The division, indeed, the multiplication of matter is thus shown as one of the foundations of the signifying function (Kristeva 1984).

A vertiginous foundation, to be sure, that is in the a-symbolic and a-signifiable infinite nothingness of speculative philosophy: a foundation in a cut, a scission, a void, a Heraclitean division without beginning or end. What makes this ultimate hiatus work is its return: the repetition, the reiteration, the multiplicity of rupture. The chora retains its renovating capacity only through this rhythm of splitting and separation. Kristeva's reference to the world of quanta and nucleic acids as scientific myths and not as science's indisputable claims to mastery, and her evocation of a vertiginous world of infinite splitting make us posit an other of gender. The fundamental instability and uncertainty of the maternal/paternal duality and its ultimate disappearance in the cut of the splitting cell come as a reminder that, besides the problematic gender difference, there is also the problematic difference between gender and nongender. To posit an other of gender, then, is to posit stars or protozoa from which we differ insofar as we differ between ourselves.

Hence there is a limit to the concerns in this text, a limit punctured by protozoa and stars. If we have to be precise, it is in the cut of this limit that the text hangs. If the symbolic and its syntax are the occultation of sexual difference, if the signifier functions through the exclusion of woman, then language is another way to mark the same limit. Between these two, in the nothingness between the genderless word and the genderless star, our endeavor that has nevertheless to use language and to cast a glance from time to time to the stars unfolds. It is flanked by Urania, the muse of astronomy, of the Big Bang of the expanding, forever lost maternal body, and by Osiris, the mummified phallus of the paternal word. But what of a living and loving father? A child is said to have been conceived lately by way of a star ray that entered the father through the eye—a new wonder of the world. "There are these other forms of life, artificial ones, that want to come into existence. And they are using me as a vehicle for its reproduction and its implementation."[5] Is it to the impending cry of this child born of logic that we haste to its plea for a body?

The question is, If the phallus has taken, theoretically, the place of the logos, whatever could be the reality that this shift inverts? This study refers to asymmetrical temporalities and loves that can be subsumed under the categories of male and female libidos, of love in the shadow of the phallus (as Kristeva has it), and of love in the shadow of the mother (as Woolf's *To the Lighthouse* enables me to say it). Yet all our loves are already in the shadow of the machine, and it is in this shadow that I try to situate my question. Is the rigor of playing sufficient to sustain the metaphysics of the body?

To put it differently, is the whole exertion of writing the body a way of witnessing the body's disappearance? Does the effort to recuperate the mother from mystery into the exigencies of the symbolic, into an imaginary father that envelops and holds, does this effort mark the dawn of an epoch in which motherhood will be no less fictive than fatherhood, an epoch whose children will be parented from the realms of the invisible protozoa? Children who, rather than engender the formula—to paraphrase one of Kristeva's titles—will be engendered and embraced by it? Does the toil to en-gender language amount to a plea for the ludic preservation of sexual differences and their troubles in a future that may no longer need them? Does this plea transpose the playful en-gendering into an utmost seriousness concerning the very basis of our sociality? Or is woman's word finally summoned to this end—to convey to language a corporeality that will dissolve on this side in order to be handed over there to cyborgs? Yet it is doubtful that this fantastic need, this fantastic supplication reversing the request of Andersen's "Little Mermaid," arises at all to fill the universe with its ghostly shivering. Give me a body, Mother; make me mortal so that I can love! The Little Mermaid had to struggle for her soul through pain but to this uncanny solicitor we shall say: Read! The rhythm is thy body, the syntax will embrace thee.

---

5. The words belong to an artificial life expert (Levy 1992, p. 120).

2

The Lost Territory: The Polylogue as a Novel

In this chapter I will read Kristeva's theory as a novel. The possibility for such a reading is suggested by Kristeva's own chosen term *polylogue*, as discussed in the previous chapter, where the polylogue can be seen as a transposition of Bakhtin's polyphony into the problematic heterogeneity of theoretical writing. The polylogic reading allows me to follow Kristeva's interdisciplinary work along the trajectory of a secret narrative: the narrative of an irrecoverable lost territory, of an immortal sorrow, of a disconsolate wandering. Parables of exile, trajectories of exile. Turns of strangeness where the theoretical movement toward a forever lost object returns as the narrative—the fiction, the parabolic curve—of a flight away from that object. As the parabola of foreignness, in a word. Is it because "the transposition of the 'sovereign operation' in language requires a *literature* and not philosophy or knowledge" (Kristeva 1977, p. 117)? Within this inverted movement, the problem of the polylogue emerges as the problem of a literary genre.

To treat theory in terms of the stories it tells is an approach that hardly needs justification nowadays. It is important to note, however, that such an approach is indispensable in light of Kristeva's own comments. Her theoretical discourse undergoes a deliberate fictionalization, which becomes more explicit and evident with each new book. Thus the temptation of "literary or para-literary fiction," which is resisted in the preface to *Desire in Language* (Kristeva 1980, p. ix), turns into an inescapable "share of fiction" in *Powers of Horror* (Kristeva 1982, p. 68). Later on her project is described as resembling "narrative fiction"; as, ultimately, close to literature and art in its ambition to "restore to illusion its full therapeutic and epistemological value" (Kristeva 1987a, pp. 19, 21) and its cathartic effect (Kristeva 1989).

With *The Samurai*, Kristeva's writing eventually crossed the borderline beyond which it could define itself as "novel." What I shall be interested in, however, is the deferral of this crossing, the hovering on the border. Kristeva's theoretical writing does not topple over completely either into fiction, or, on the other hand, into metaphysics, toward which it nevertheless veers. This is attributed in her own comments to the ability of psychoanalytic discourse to produce a certain knowledge effect, amounting to a preservation of the typology of discourses, that is, of the lucid distinctness of the voices (poetical, philosophical, analytical) in Kristeva's polylogue (Kristeva 1987b). Thus psychoanalytic discourse plays the role of "analyst" to Kristeva's generic heterogeneity, interpreting this heterogeneity in the very poetic and mimetic act that produces it. Genre itself turns into an "analysand" very similar to the protagonist of Kristeva's "fiction": an exile who asks "Where?," a restless wanderer obsessed with drawing boundaries and dividing spaces, a wearer of masks playing with multiple identities, a melancholy stray traversing a forever foreign country.

THE SILENT SISTER OF PHILOSOPHY

The key position held by psychoanalytic discourse as the "discourse of discourses" in Kristeva's polylogic economy of genre, however, is only seemingly secure and established. As a theoretical discourse incarnated by poetic mimesis into other types of discourse, it confirms its interpretative primacy only by the effective cure, that is, by a gesture that goes beyond interpretation and, for that matter, beyond speech. Kristeva calls this gesture a "lucid wakening of lovers"—a creation of "love's time and space" (Kristeva 1987b, pp. 233, 323), a *rebirth*. The psychoanalytic discourse, therefore, is realized only through slipping away from itself, through a movement that opens up a utopian space where the reborn individual confronts the challenge of the empty sky.

If on its "far side" (one of Kristeva's favorite topological distinctions) analytic discourse dissolves into a creative act, into a polyvalent utopian health, on the "near side" it hovers above the silence of suffering and pain. "My suffering is the lining of my speech, of my civilization" (Kristeva 1989, p. 182). "My sorrow is the hidden face of my philosophy, her mute sister" (p. 4). The mute sister is the sorrowful double, the hidden face of philosophy, speech, civilization—a silence that is always there, beyond any articulation of meaning, beyond, therefore, the whole range of the typology of discourses.

Commenting on the function of alchemy in the poetry of Nerval—a key figure in Kristeva's theatre of masks—Kristeva points out that the esoteric doctrine with its rigid symbolicity is added to the polyvalent order of the poetic. This leads to "a twofold advantage: on the one hand, insuring a stable meaning as well as a secret community where the disconsolate poet is heard, accepted and, in short, solaced; on the other, slipping away from that monovalent meaning and that same community in order to reach as closely as possible the specifically Nervalian object, sorrow—and this through traversing the uncertainty of naming" (Kristeva 1989, p. 147).

In a similar way, Kristeva's analytic discourse, lined with its own project of amorous transmutation and constantly unsettled by poetic mimesis, slips away from its rigid vocabulary in order to approach, across the uncertainty of naming, the hidden face of a silent double: Kristeva's specific object of exile and loss. It is the "hidden sister" that really interests her, the mute story under the cover of a borrowed language.

THE EXILE IN LANGUAGE

Throughout her works, Julia Kristeva elaborates the enigmatic foundations of the oedipal triangle: a stage logically and chronologically prior to the patricidal oedipal trope. An inarticulate oceanic unity ("a community of dolphins")—a rather feminine element of lethal and jubilatory indistinctness—precedes the male strife in Freud's primary horde. This is the place or no-place where the power of the archaic mother holds sway; the power of a blissful and stifling embrace before the emergence of subjectivity, signification, and meaning. The threat that the archaic mother presents is of a total loss of self rather than of castration; and the necessity of *matricide* faces the would-be speaking being as the only way toward subjectivity and language.

The violent nature of this necessity is emphasized by the impossibility of incorporation or integration of the murdered mother (in the way the father, in Freud, is incorporated by the murderous brothers through eating the totem). Matricide, on the contrary, is realized as "vomiting" the maternal body, as rejecting it. This rejection draws the first boundary between inside and outside, it is the first line separating a still fragile "I" from "everything else." "I feel like vomiting the mother" (Kristeva 1982, p. 47): this metaphor of reverse creation names an archaic creative act that establishes the first boundary, the first precarious measurement of space, and the primal irrecoverable loss. There is something drastically final about the necessity of rejecting the mother; according to Kristeva, civilization and phallic idealization are founded on the putting to death of the feminine body.

Deprivation initiates the entry of the speaking being into language. The advent into language is seen as the establishment of a map that divides the territory of the speaking subject from the invisible maternal continent. The expulsion of the mother becomes a self-expulsion and the speaking being is neither guided nor born, but expelled into language. Language unfolds like a foreign country out of the loss of the motherland; it is always a language of want, of lack; a translation of the missing mother, of the nothingness of an object that has always already been lost. It is emptiness that produces signification and subjectivity.

The speaking being is constituted, therefore, *as an exile*. S/he is haunted by a "past that does not pass by" (Kristeva 1989, p. 60), by "forgetfulness and thunder in a *land of oblivion* that is constantly remembered" (Kristeva 1982, p. 8). By a series of separations, through a "vertiginous course towards metalanguages or foreign languages" (Kristeva 1989, p. 42), further and further away from the pain of the lost paradise, s/he becomes a deviser of new territories and new languages, a producer and reconstructor of culture. This is the only choice, the destiny of the speaking being. If the vertiginous march is arrested by an incomplete separation from the lost maternal continent, melancholy, paralysis of the signifying function, and death follow. It is only by *translating the mother* that we live: "orphans but creators, creators but forsaken" (Kristeva 1989, p. 181).

Exile is the eternal destiny of the speaking being. S/he can't go back home. The initial expulsion that constituted the leap into language and subjectivity can only be repeated, never undone, if we are to continue to speak. Each creative strategy is an elaboration of nostalgia, but at the same time it is a movement further and further away from the site of the primeval loss. The very impulse to go back multiplies the territories and the distances, thrusts us further and further into space.

In this way, together with Mallarmé, whom Kristeva quotes repeatedly throughout her work, Kristeva's speaking being seems to restate, that "nothing shall have taken place but the place" (Kristeva 1982, p. 138). The astronomer's Muse, Urania, the Muse of the point in space, the Muse of emptiness and mathematical precision, presides over the *history* of the speaking being. This history is "only spatial variation" (Kristeva 1980, p. 281); it is a history of confronting new spaces *as* new ways of speaking.[1]

It is the story of *Oedipus at Colonus*, of Oedipus *the exile*, that Kristeva adds to the Freudian version of *Oedipus Rex*. Only as an exile does Oedipus leave his incestuous royalty and find himself as subject to the Law and the Symbolic. The speaking being dwells in language as an exile. With Kristeva, language is the homelessness of being.

THE CHORA

As I already pointed out in the previous chapter, Kristeva's elaboration of the archaic mother's power provoked much controversy in feminist literature. In its double, but equally speechless, aspect of abjection and sublimity, of hell and jouissance, carrion and paradise, this unnameable primeval space was frequently discussed by Kristeva "intersexually" via male artistic practice. This led to a common feeling that "in a further echo of Freudian phallocentrism, Kristeva's encoding of the artist/child privileges the male to the detriment of the female" (Stanton 1986, pp. 166–167). Such a theorizing of the mother is in obvious contradiction with her empirical role as a first language teacher, and with the very notion of *mother* tongue. It was read by Kaja Silverman (1988) as a complete "writing out of the maternal" (p. 119), which, together with Kristeva's preference for male artists, could be seen as a defense mechanism motivated by a homosexual desire for the mother. A strange unawareness it must have been, on Kristeva's part, of one of her own theoretical premises. This premise posits the gigantic difficulty, for woman, of finding a heterosexual object of love (Kristeva 1989). It decodes the act of giving birth as a phantasmatic reunion of the mother

---

1. The metamorphosis of Urania into a Muse of exiles belongs to Joseph Brodsky (Brodskii 1987, p. 63).

with the body of *her* mother, and the demand for a penis as fantasy's sign for the yearning to reach the mother (Kristeva 1980). It regards the incestuous desire for the father as a substitution for the desire for the mother, as in the reading, in *Tales of Love*, of Dante's condemnation of Myrrha (Kristeva 1987b). Kristeva is convinced that female homosexuality is endogenous (Kristeva 2002a). Alice Jardine (1986), on the other hand, found that "it was the Male-Subject-Creative-of-Our-Dominant-*and*-Marginal-culture that Kristeva was going to x-ray—building a sort of inventory of possible male libidinal economies" (p. 110). Silverman saw unconscious desire where Jardine found a calculated political strategy.

Much of the controversy over Kristeva's treatment of the maternal problematic was centered around the question of the chora. In *The Revolution in Poetic Language* (1984), Kristeva introduces this term from Plato's *Timaeus* in a manner that seems, at least at first glance, straightforward and unproblematic. Supporting her definition of the chora with quotations from *Timaeus*, she describes it as a dynamic space beyond representation, unstable, uncertain, and full of commotion, as, in the last analysis, unnameable. Before deciding, however, as Jacqueline Rose (1986) does, that Plato's reduction of motherhood to passive receptivity is part of Kristeva's concept of the chora and of the feminine, it is worth examining whether the introduction of Plato's term is as direct as it might seem.

The belief that the mother does not actually take part in procreation, and that she is only the "nurse" of the unborn child, is part of the effort of Greek culture of that time to erase all hints of matriarchal power. Aeschylus's *Oresteia* is a famous example. With her craving for power, Clytemnestra is represented as a chthonic monster who is rightfully killed by her children, precisely because a mother is not a "parent." Even with Plato, however, the nonparticipation of the Receptacle (or chora) in the "clinging to existence" of the "copies," of the world of Becoming, has some strange consequences. The Receptacle stands in Plato's cosmology as an independent power, everlasting and unchanging like the divine itself. It "does not owe its existence to the Demiurge, but is represented as a given factor limiting his actions by necessary conditions" (Cornford 1956, p. 193).

Equivocal as it is in Plato's work, this term is subjected to a number of transformations in Kristeva's writing. The first difference is, of course, that Plato's term is taken out of its cosmogonic frame and related to the analytic trope of the advent of the speaking being. The cosmogonic problematic does indeed open up in the void of infinite scission, but it also vanishes there in order to return as the narrative of the speaking being.

What remains of this problematic is the question of priority. Although this question is marked by the *aion*, by an insoluble hermeneutic circularity, in Kristeva's theoretical reconstruction the logical and chronological priority is given to the chora (Kristeva 1982, 1984, 1987a). In the beginning, therefore, is *not* the Word, not the Logos; in the beginning is Love, the generative chora. With Kristeva, the chora is the dynamic principle that, through the archaic power of the maternal "Receptacle," compensates for the fragility and "impotence" of the symbolic (the Logos). The eternity and primacy of the Logos is drawn from an underlying reliance on the maternal that sustains it (Kristeva 1987b).

Kristeva's chora is neither characterless as it is in Plato, nor a mere container of chaos as it is in *Timaeus* before the interference of the Demiurge. It is a rhythmical ordering of the semiotic—"echolalic, vocalizing, lilting, gestural, muscular" (Kristeva 1987b, p. 126). It is an agent not only in the dynamics that thrust the speaking being into language and subjectivity, but also in the constant creative unsettlement of the symbolic by the semiotic. Displacing Plato's Demiurge, it becomes the troubled source of demiurgic activity.

Far from offering an ontological grounding, Kristeva's chora becomes part of a signifying process that is "the only concrete universality that defines the speaking being" (Kristeva 1982, p. 67); a signifying process carried out over emptiness. In her recent writing Kristeva takes this idea one step further through the conceptualization—via Plato's myth of the cave from the *Republic*—of the autistic body as the "cave" of pure sensation, of dreamless sleep. The autistic body thus marks the zero degree of the signifying process that can be put in motion only by the orderings of the chora (Kristeva 1996).

The notion of emptiness underlying signifying structures marks another dissociation from the Platonic project: Kristeva's speaking being is not after absolute truth but after "a little more truth, an impossible truth" (Kristeva 1980, p. ix). In a movement that relocates Plato's Eros into the exigencies of transference love, the Platonic dialogic maieusis of truth is transposed into the polylogic articulation of rebirth. Kristeva's speaking being is enunciated, via the lucid wakening of lovers, as a quest through shifting identities that resist stability and are thus a perpetuation of exile. The truth of the speaking being is the effective cure, a gesture toward the corporeal, unleashing the human capacities for innovation.

The chora is, in the last analysis, the carrier of logical and chronological primacy in the becoming of the speaking being, of whatever immortality or eternity is humanly conceivable, of truth as wandering, renewal and rebirth, and of artistic creativity. Kristeva's argument, therefore, is situated on this side of the Platonic universe where souls are not exiled from the realm of Forms into the sublunar *Simulacra*. Rather, they are incorporated into language; nourishing themselves with words, they leap from the chora into language.

Thus the chora is not a matter of a simple transfer from Plato. Seen in the framework of Kristeva's preoccupation with the destiny of the speaking being, it obviously does not amount to a writing out of the maternal. The story of Kristeva's deplatonizing of the Platonic concept, however, leaves one question unanswered.

LANGUAGE AS A MASK

This story obviously reinforces the notion of exile into language as the destiny of the speaking being (as opposed to the exile in the corporeal world, which is part of the Platonic tradition). And yet, why chora? Wherefore χώρα? Why Plato? Why, in other words, a term *with a history*? And, still more puzzlingly, why a word with a history, if this history is then surreptitiously undone?

The chora is, in fact, only one among numerous examples. Kristeva's early writing is full of heterogeneous terms, often drawn from the most unlikely sources. It sometimes leaves the impression of an elaborate cipher. In one essay only ("The Bounded Text"), she borrows terms from such a variegated assembly of authors as Bakhtin (*ideologeme*), Greimas (*sememe*), Quine (his *reification of universals*), Shklovski (*loop*), von Wright (*alethic, deontic*), Tesnière (*junctive, translative*), etc. (Kristeva 1980). Her later works grow more restrained, and yet drastically transplanted words continue to appear, introducing the flavor of different metalanguages, of foreign tongues, and exotic alphabets.

"The Bounded Text" was published in a book whose title is representative of this tendency: Σημειωτικὴ. The Greek word, whose exotic nature is made more emphatic by rendering it with the Greek letters, contains a tacit reference to a journal bearing precisely the same title, Σημειωτικὴ with just the diacritic mark tracing an enigmatic differentiation but also, possibly, a mysterious visual bridge. The journal was launched in 1964 by the Tartu-Moscow semiotic school of Jurii Lotman (whom Kristeva quotes in her book along with many other representatives of East European theory) and hence amplifies the invocation of the Greek letters with other scripts and languages. The exotic word is then translated by a neologism: *semanalysis*. The aim of semanalysis is to describe "signifying phenomena, while analyzing, criticizing, and dissolving 'phenomenon,' 'meaning,' and 'signifier'"(Kristeva 1980, p. vii).

Is the violent introduction of "aliens" among the natives of the language part of this project? Seen in the light of Kristeva's later work, it is obviously an instance of the "vertiginous course towards metalanguages or foreign languages," (Kristeva 1989, p. 42) which is the destiny of the human being. It is an example of that indefatigable translation of the mother, which draws us further and further away from her. It emphasizes the necessary foreignness of language. Kristeva's typologies of the speaking being are always in the long run typologies of exile. They are inescapably situated between the gravitation of the lost territory, simultaneously invisible and dazzling, and the weightless awareness of the emptiness of language. For the subject of abjection the words are permeated "with nonexistence, with a hallucinatory, ghostly glimmer" (Kristeva 1982, p. 6). And the speech of the depressed is a "mask—a beautiful facade carved out of a 'foreign language'" (Kristeva 1989, p. 55).

This awareness of language as a facade without a building, of language as a flimsy make-believe permeated by nothingness, is not only discussed but also enacted in Kristeva's polylogue. Terms like the *chora*, behind which the whole history of Occidental ideas can sometimes stand, get hollowed out through a corrosive use, through a violence that exhibits their arbitrariness. A strange "thinning" of language is revealed—a precarious transparency beyond which a bifurcation of spaces opens. One is the space of darkness, of forgetfulness and stasis, of the melancholic sister of philosophy. The other is the space of the unessential man, of the comedian, the *mask*.

DOUBLES AND PSEUDONYMS

Throughout her works after *Polylogue*, Kristeva creates a whole typology of exiles. She transposes their disconsolate homelessness into a Dantesque vertical and atemporal vision—an exile's vision to be sure—of unspeakable suffering and ecstasy. In this way, Kristeva provides another instance of the polylogic dimension of her writing. The abject is "an exile who asks 'Where?'"; who "*strays* instead of getting her bearings"; who defines herself

by "Where am I?" instead of "Who am I?"; who keeps separating herself
from her never forgotten land of oblivion (Kristeva 1982, p. 8). In *Tales of
Love* Narcissus, the antihero of Kristeva's history of the human psyche, is
"an exile deprived of his psychic space, an extraterrestrial with a prehistory bearing" (Kristeva 1987b, p. 382). In *Black Sun* the melancholic is "a
stranger in her mother tongue" (Kristeva 1989, p. 53). The different destinies of the speaking subject converge in their common horizon of exile.

When names appear to render concreteness to Kristeva's typologi-
cal exiles, these names often turn out to be pseudonyms. Kristeva's protagonists share, besides a lost territory and a foreign language, a frequent
uncertainty regarding their name and identity. Céline is a pseudonym;
Stendhal is a pseudonym; Nerval is a pseudonym. They are further shown
through an identification and doubling, which they undergo in their texts.
Céline identifies himself with the subject of his doctoral dissertation, Ignaz
Semmelweis, a Hungarian doctor practicing in Vienna. Stendhal is noto-
rious for his love of mystification and disguise, his polyglottism, his fascination with the distant and the foreign. And Nerval enacts a "dispersal
of the 'I,' loving as well as poetic, into a constellation of elusive identities" (Kristeva 1989, p. 157). Masquerade accomplishes the situation of
the exile.

It is noteworthy that this play at redoubling includes, with Kristeva's
protagonists, the splitting of female doubles from the male artists. *Céline*
is a female name, the name of the writer's grandmother, and it is under
this name that he writes his novels. *Nerval* is an anagram of the maiden
name of the poet's mother. For one reason or another, Céline and Nerval
have chosen "the Name of the Mother." In his sonnet *Artémis*, Nerval ren-
ders a masculine form to the name of Artemisia and "perhaps plays with
the two members of the couple as if each were the *double* of the other—
interchangeable but also, consequently, imprecise in their sexuality"
(Kristeva 1989, p. 148).

The *redoubling* of Artemis is interpreted as an equivalent of Nerval's
poem itself. The polylogue of elusive identities, the intersexual encrypting
of the other in oneself, and the ensuing splitting of masks become equivalent to the oeuvre. The oeuvre is this playful splitting, this confrontation
of doubles. If Kristeva's description of Nerval's poem is applied to her own
writing, it can reveal a multiple refraction of perspectives at work. In *Black
Sun* the "lost territory" is first telescoped through Holbein's painting of the
dead Christ whose death is depicted beyond all hope precisely because

Mary, the maternal upholder of the promise for resurrection, is conspicuously absent. The painting is then shown as seen by Myshkin, the hero of Dostoevsky's *The Idiot*. Myshkin's experience of the picture leads to the troubled response of Dostoevsky himself and to the story about this response as seen and interpreted by Anna Grigorievna, Dostoevsky's wife.

Further, a proximity between the theoretician and the object of study seems to be at work as a device mirroring the creative process itself. At the heart of *Black Sun* Nerval is writing his poem about melancholy with the famous image of the black sun that has given the title to Kristeva's book about melancholy. Nerval is one of Kristeva's exiles: a restless traveler rent by a hidden grief that he interprets as nostalgia, as the sorrow for a lost territory that cannot be forgotten. This memory, which deprives him of the future, makes him be what he is not (for he is the memory of a loss, of a lack, of an absence): a man with a mask, with a pseudonym; a man with elusive identity, with feminine doubles. He is, further, fascinated with esoteric codes (alchemy) or foreign languages, which is reminiscent of Kristeva's own fascination and which is interpreted by her as yet another sign of redoubling; the recourse to different languages is seen as a recourse to different identities. The title of his poem, in a fashion suggestive of some of Kristeva's titles, is *El Desdichado*, a strangely sounding linguistic alien, a Spanish word that has reached Nerval via Lesage, Scott, and Dumas, a "masked" word with a history, including translations, fictional shifts, and misinterpretations. This history is discussed by Kristeva, and as a result, the word is made to mean not quite what it means. It keeps something of its dictionary meaning as "unhappy" and "miserable," but at the same time it acquires the very specific sense of "disinherited," thus pointing once again at the lost territory. Nerval is as concerned with "an unnamable territory, which one could evoke or invoke, strangely, from a strange land, from a constitutive exile" (Kristeva 1989, p. 145), as Kristeva's theory itself. He seems to be redoubling her own creative endeavor.

Thus *Black Sun* might be read as the striking history of the effort of a melancholy theoretician, actually introduced in the book (Kristeva 1989) to weave a narrative out of stasis and out of her initial question how one can at all speak about melancholy if melancholy is, in the first place, a paralysis of the ability to speak. The answer then comes through encrypting and redoubling with others who have made the same effort and who mirror the creation of the book. Once again the problematic of exile as a vertiginous march from one language to another and from one identity to another is not only discussed but also refracted and enacted in the process of writing itself.

BORN FROM THE HEAD

A famous amorous wearer of masks is none other than Zeus himself. He is the lover with a thousand bodies: a bull, a swan, or rain of gold. He is also the god who, in the story of Western culture, made the most explicit effort to expropriate birth-giving. On one occasion, he swallowed the goddess of wisdom, Metis, who was pregnant; thus, after her mother was swallowed, Athena was born from the head of her father. On another occasion, he was asked by Semele to reveal to her his real appearance; she was annihilated by the spectacle and her prematurely born child had to be sewn in the thigh of Zeus until the proper time came—that is how Dionysus was born. Or, as Kristeva (1987b) reminds us, "phallic power . . . would in short begin with an appropriation of archaic maternal power" (p. 75).

To this could be added that (1) the appropriation of generative power is effected as a simultaneous appropriation of sight; (2) mask, disguise, the right to invisibility are constituted as the prerogative of the one who sees; and (3) by appropriating the functions of both father and mother, Zeus appropriates the authorship of the whole of culture in its entire range from the verge of the natural and the ecstatic (Dionysus) to the urban and the intellectual (Athena), and in its masculine as well as feminine aspects—both Dionysus and Athena have markedly androgynous traits.

What should not be forgotten, therefore—and this is what Kristeva's works emphatically remind us—is that the desire to "vomit" the mother comes from the fact of her being "swallowed" in the first place. They remind us that, in Zeus, there is a *swallowed mother*; that, in culture, *maternity has remained unknown*. From Socrates's maieusis to the contemporary scientist who sees himself as the vehicle of eager artificial forms of life, the Muse of the "strange transvestism of the male poet giving birth to his own voice" (Harvey 1992, p. 79) has presided over the simultaneous appropriation and denial of femininity. The quest for the mother, the obsession with translating an anonymous lost territory, with externalizing a hidden unnameable presence, thus turns into a historical gesture that, with Kristeva, can be effected only by accepting the necessity of mediation, of rebirth from the "head" of a culture signed with the Name of the Father and yet containing in itself its *mater abscondita*.

This is, I believe, the background of Kristeva's redoublings, of her male masquerade and of her intersexual dynamic. The masquerade indicates a decentered doer who never coincides with the doing. It is with regard to the god—or to the perfect marionette—that we cannot tell the dancer from the dance. As with Heinrich von Kleist's never perfect human dancer, the mask marks a center of gravity that is always in the wrong place exhibiting the split with which the speaking subject begins and from which the very possibility for questioning and rebellion springs. Lined with the silence of anonymous female suffering and with the laughter of male masks, Kristeva's (1987b) polylogue offers its solution of "shattering identification" (p. 201). The acceptance of the mask, of the *principle* of masking, is an entry to a utopia of opening spaces, of multiplication of the universe, of undecidability and interminable questioning: a meticulous proliferation of identities, a gradual reinvestment of new *readiness* for meaning, a reappropriation of the chora of creation. It is the transformation of exile into a quest, into a figure of infinity. Exile turns out to be not only the constitutive beginning and the eternal destiny of the speaking being, but also its "polytopic" goal as well, a liberating gesture under the empty skies.

BELLINI REVISITED

Kristeva's works have to be entered as one enters a hall of mirrors; the doubling and mirroring, the play of masks and of reflections is the medium of her polylogue, which as a genre is, too, a multiple splitting of discourse. Besides the utopian centrifugal movement, besides the polytopic opening of spaces through the laughter of masking and play, the splitting involves an opposite movement, a movement toward silence, pain, and inarticulate stasis, toward the hidden sister of philosophy. In this refracting light, which is part of Kristeva's (1982) multiplication of spaces, a rereading of "Motherhood According to Giovanni Bellini" might offer additional insight into Kristeva's polylogic theory. It is a threshold essay not only in terms of Kristeva's own work, signaling as it does the preoccupations of her later writing, but also in terms of its problematic posited on the threshold of two epochs, of the Eastern and the Western Rome and of two possibilities open to Western culture, of which *one* has been chosen.

"Motherhood According to Giovanni Bellini" provides, therefore, a specific cultural and historical frame to Kristeva's introduction of the theme of the lost maternal territory. This frame is elaborated to a great extent in geographical terms, by an emphasis on the unique position of Venice as an offspring of Byzantine culture—a city looking both East and West, a historical crossroad. The lack of sufficient knowledge about Bellini is thus partly compensated for by a geographical pattern that locates the brief hope of a jouissant culture, a culture that sprang from the East before the East itself was thwarted and rejected.

The spatial dimension is emphasized once again by the theme of exile. The contrast between Bellini and Leonardo da Vinci is explicit and has been discussed by Kristeva's commentators (Jacobus 1986). The doubling of Bellini and Dante, however, seems to have remained unnoticed. Dante, who usually figures in Kristeva's writing as the author of the most exalted transposition of the mother–son incest, shares Bellini's dazzling vision. Many intellectuals during the Middle Ages and especially during the Renaissance spent their life wandering from one place to another. Dante, however, is a passionate exile. His *Comedia* is attributed to his banishment, which forced him to give up the heated political struggles in his native city. His journey crowned with the radiant heavenly spheres can be seen as emerging from his loss, the way Bellini's luminous spaces are seen by Kristeva as arising from a hypothetical motherlessness.

The luminosity itself is related by Kristeva (1980), among other things, to the "pagan-matriarchal Orientalism" (p. 243) and the "revealing Orthodox conception" (p. 251) of the Virgin as privileged space: *ergasterion*. The theorizing of the mother both in terms of losing her (exile) and of surrogating her, acquiring her in sublime joy where she is not, is thus carried out here, as elsewhere in Kristeva's works, through exile and geography, through drawing maps and creation of spaces, and through the temptations of polyglottism.

In sketching the facets of Byzantine culture and art that probably intersected with Western humanism, giving their unique results in Bellini's Madonnas, Kristeva mentions a few names: the frescoes in Sopocani, Serbia, and *Our Lady of Vladimir*, a remarkable work created in Constantinople around 1125–1130 and transferred to Kiev. However brief it may be, this sketch outlines the two important developments that Byzantium transmitted to the West in terms of art: the elaborate composition of the Sopocani frescoes and the humanistic compassion (*umilenie, heleousia*) manifested in *Our Lady of Vladimir*. It also draws a broad trajectory that cuts across the Byzantine cultural sphere and surrounds a certain unmentioned space: Bulgaria.

Kristeva's position as an exile from Bulgaria has often been discussed, although in rather contradictory terms. As mentioned earlier, she was described as both unconscious about what she writes and as politically calculating. In a similar manner, she is seen, on the one hand, as hegemonically central. According to Gayatri Spivak (1988), "her own pre-history in Bulgaria is not even a shadow under the harsh light of the Parisian voice" (p. 140). On the other hand, she is perceived as flaunting her marginality, as a "vulgar Bulgar" (Gallop 1982, p. 120).

Bulgaria was part of the Byzantine cultural sphere. A fascination with the splendors and the sophistication of Constantinople and with Byzantine spirituality seemed to survive the fall of the Eastern Roman Empire itself, and the temptations and the threats of Greek culture persisted long after the two countries had been conquered by the Turks. Bulgaria shared the specific Eastern Orthodox preoccupation with the cult of Mother of God. An apocrypha about the descent of Mary in hell, which is one of the possible sources for Dante's *Comedia*, was among the most widely read texts in medieval Bulgarian literature.

To the Orthodox emphasis on the *Mother of God*, Bulgarian folklore added a pervasive concern with the mother–*daughter* relationship. This relationship is described in paradisical terms as dazzling sunshine, flower-picking, and bliss. There are no men in this spring world of singing and dancing, of bright colors and laughter. Men appear only to put an end to it; marriage is seen as the inevitable coming of winter, erasing beauty, youth, happiness, and freedom at one blow. Thus a pattern resembling the Demeter–Persephone myth seems to emerge out of this mother–daughter paradise threatened by the male world.[2]

---

2. The following example is typical; it is noteworthy that the text of the song never explicitly mentions the separation from the mother or marriage: the spring–winter contrast and the extinction of the sun in a "stranger's house" are considered explicit enough.

> The sun is shining in Neda's garden,
> o willow-tree, o willow tree.
> It is not the clear sun shining,
> it is Neda herself, Neda herself:
> her black eyes like a doe's,
> her eyelashes like sweet basil,
> her teeth like white pearls,
> her body like a wood-nymph's.
> The young maidens have gathered
> to dance on the green grass,
> to pick up yellow flower,
> to bask in the warm sun.

The question is, Is there, perhaps, a hidden map in the geography of "Motherhood According to Giovanni Bellini"? Are the outlines of the lost territory, of the darkened maternal space possibly given? Is the image of the Virgin, which, according to Kristeva's (1987a) own story, sat enthroned above her bed in adolescence and fascinated her with the mysterious grace of Byzantine iconography—is that image perhaps veiled behind Bellini's Madonnas? Is, in a backward vertiginous march, the Bulgarian meaning of *people* or *dance* "echoing" and "vocalizing" through the *chora*, χώρα, xopa? And the paradisical union with the mother sustaining a repression that is quite secondary?

In fact, one wonders whether this is a repression at all. Above I outlined the contradictions between Silverman (unconscious desire) and Jardine (calculated political strategy), Spivak (not a shadow of the past) and Gallop (flaunting marginality) in the discussions of Kristeva. The very disparity of these views suggests that the voice of marginality tends to be perceived as an oscillation between the inaudible and the vulgar. We always seem to have too much (the vulgar Bulgar) or too little (the hegemonic Parisian) of the marginal; in either case, we cannot quite hear it. Coming back to Kristeva's essay, we can see that Bellini's incestuous jouissance is framed by an "excursion to the limits of primal regression [which] can be phantasmatically experienced as the reunion of a woman-mother with the body of *her* mother" (Kristeva 1980, p. 239). The story of Bellini's (surrogating) recovery of the lost mother is after that unfolded as surrogation of that other story, the story about the mother and the daughter. This story moreover, is a parable about the surrogation of the East by the West, of the "marginal" by the "central." The very surrogation, however, is a way of telling the erased story. In writing the essay, Kristeva is performing Bellini's creative act. Bellini's luminous Madonnas were his method for surrogating the

---

Neda tells them in a whisper,
"Listen to me, young maidens,
bask in the dear warm sun
before it is burnt out,
before there starts to blow
a fierce winter in a stranger's house." [anonymous; translation mine]

The second half of the song, in which Neda (sorrowful, careworn, and obviously already married) addresses "three hundred lads" who are breaking the branches of the willow tree, is even darker. After reading this text Kristeva told me that this song was the favorite song of her father.

mother. Kristeva's writing about the male artist is *her* method for a similar surrogation. As a result, the mother–daughter relationship subtends the story of the male artist and his mother. Bellini as an object of Kristeva's study is hence her double, and the redoubling explores the infinite paradox that the mute sister of philosophy presents to language.

What should be added, therefore, is a hidden map, a hidden icon showing through Venice and Bellini's Madonnas. The darkening of this map, which bursts on the far side of language into serene iridescent spaces, hints at the ways in which Kristeva speaks of darkness through luminosity, of silence through polyglottism, and of the hidden face through masks.

3

Strangers' Games: The Polylogue in a Utopian Perspective

DER SPIELTRIEB

The exploration of the maternal presence in language brings Julia Kristeva to the problem of the "imaginary father," the phantasm of a father who can love like a mother. It is precisely the lack of a loving father that can explain, according to Kristeva, the crisis of the modern soul, and not the lack of a stern and relentless patriarch as it is sometimes claimed. The concept of the imaginary father is intellectually derived from Hegel, Freud, and Lacan, but it is imaginatively drawn from the maternal aura of the Eastern Orthodox Trinity, an aura that Kristeva nostalgically transplants under the empty skies of the modern soul.[1] Bringing together some persistent utopian traits of Kristeva's writing, the concept is a solicitation to revisit the watery settings of Narcissus in order to gaze at the *image*. This gazing has to be free of Narcissus's illusions, however. It has to be aware of the irreality of the image, and of the reality of our love for the fake.

---

1. For an analogy between the imaginary father and the Eastern Orthodox Trinity, see the chapter on Dostoevsky in *Black Sun* (Kristeva 1989).

The phantom loveliness of our own creations once produced the space of the Western psyche and today, according to Kristeva, could become the wager for a new humanity.

The imaginary—maternal—father thus reverberates Schiller's defense of "mere appearance." He is the guarantee of a ludic entry into the oedipal triangle and provides a theatrical setting for the becoming of the subject: of the subject as a game of I-s (*jeu de jes*), as a gambling of the I-s, or as an I-dice as I shall presently call it. The imaginary father promises aesthetic salvation through the virtues of the seeming. Thus, he allows a crucial transformation of the drives into what might be defined, in the light of Schiller's *Spieltrieb*, as "playdrives" or, indeed, as gambling drives. This utopian echo retains Freud's emphasis on the drives. Nevertheless, it insists, ever since Kristeva's conceptualization of the chora, on the perilous creativity of an unreal theatrical and protean I in the grips of a permanent crisis. In this way Kristeva's theory evokes the ludic vistas of Schiller's pedagogic and aesthetic utopianism.

These vistas are constructed as a subterfuge against emptiness and madness rather than against the repressiveness of a weakened superego. By referring to the transmutation of the drives into playdrives, and of the symbolic father into an imaginary *pater ludi*, they resist both the post-structuralist fatalism of a language that writes us without residue, as well as the Frankfurtian "eschatological-sensualist" visions of reconciliation[2]—of a mindfulness to nature that gives us back to ourselves. Kristeva's utopia is foreign to the austere and ascetic tendencies that stoic thought handed down to Western culture (and to which Foucault was finally attracted); it is, as we shall presently see, open and interactive rather than enclosed in the enlightened autarky of the soul. This utopia perpetuates its tensions and its undecidable spaces through its aspect of a ludic pedagogical technique: of a self-building method, demanding the rigor of the game. This is a utopia of self-formation understood as a discipline for playing. As a problematized rescuing of aesthetics, in a word.

---

2. Albrecht Wellmer (1991) describes Adorno's aesthetics as coming close to "an eschatological and sensualistic modulation of Schopenhauer" (p.11).

THE OEUVRE

What the *Spieltrieb* produce is not an "oeuvre" but an "I"—an "I" situated in front of, rather than behind the oeuvre. Kristeva's interest in the subject, rather than the work, as the product of the *Spieltrieb* and as the focus of utopian promise, is in line with Schiller's aesthetic pedagogy, although, of course, her solutions are far from his (sentimental or naive?) ideal of the "whole man." Schiller (1795) himself seems to regard the work of art as only a partial intimation and a "high approximation" (p. 153) to his ideal of aesthetic wholeness. As both "Nought" and a state of "Supreme reality"—a paradox to be echoed by Theodor Adorno[3]—the "aesthetic mode of the psyche" (p. 151) is what really matters. It is this treatment of the work of art, as the medium prefiguring and releasing a utopian perspective on the subject, that Kristeva's theory endorses.

Kristeva's interest in the process that produces the psyche and the subject thus leads her, via the study of the work of art, to the problem of the *je de jeu*—the ludic I. The work of art—always a work in progress for that matter—is not questioned as the frozen assortment of symptoms for the abnormality of the creative subject toiling behind it, but as the perilous transsubjective laboratory that sets this subject up in the first place.

This shift in precedence blurs the boundary between art and life through a double movement in which the oeuvre is analytically destabilized into artistic practice and the subject's coming into being is delivered as an aesthetic occurrence. Kristeva's privileging of art and the artist is thus effected through a gesture that equates art to the process of subject formation. The result is not a disappearance of the subject but an insistence on the subject's capacity for rebirth. Neither is it a disappearance of the aesthetic, but rather an attempt at its, perhaps allegorical, redemption. Hence one might speak of a ludic substratum—a purposiveness without a purpose—to the appearance of the "I." With the fading of the moral rigor of a stern superego that claims us inexorably to be, or to be one thing rather than another, the subject itself partakes in the nature of the artifice. In the I-game, the *jeu de je*. This turns the feminine—for which the "as if" of tak-

---

3. In his discussion of Samuel Beckett's *Endgame*, Adorno (1982) notes that "the repose of nothingness and that of reconciliation cannot be distinguished from each other" (p. 150).

ing on subjectivity in the phallic order is a structural necessity—into a universal condition. The "I" is a work in progress, a figurative series of transformations, a potential infinity of masks. The *oeuvre* is the artist.

THE *AZ-ZAHR*

To put it differently, the "I" is a hazard, *un hasard*, a risk, that is, and a game, a game of chance and the risk of gambling. *Der Spieltrieb*, a term for which Schiller was sometimes reproached, signified in its common use the passion for gambling. In Mallarmé's poem *Un Coup de Dés*, on which the thesis of *The Revolution in Poetic Language* relies heavily and to which Kristeva repeatedly refers in her later work, we are told that "*Un coup de dés jamais n'abolira le hasard*" (Kristeva 1974, pp. 293–311). A throw of the dice never will abolish chance (*hasard*). Or, perhaps, a throw of the dice never will abolish hazard. It deserves notice that the French *hasard* (chance), as well as the English *hazard* (risk, danger) and the Bulgarian *hazart* (хазарт, gambling), come from the Arabic word for dice or dice-game—*az-zahr*. Chance—risk—gambling. Hence "a throw of the dice (*az-zahr*) never will abolish the dice (*az-zahr*)." To throw dice is not to throw them; it is to use them as dice, to confirm them as *az-zahr*. To gamble, in short. Consequently, "a throw of the dice never will abolish gambling (*hazart*)." An act of gambling does not abolish gambling; playing with chance does not eliminate chance. It acts it. The French pronunciation of *hasard* evokes the Bulgarian *az-zar* which means literally "I-dice." *Un coup de dés jamais n'abolira le az-zar.* A throw of the dice never will abolish the I-dice: *le je-dés* (*des jes*). *Der Spieltrieb* acts the I-dice, taking a chance does not abolish the I-s. The I dies, but as the I-dice (of polytopical I-s) it gambles its paranoid numerical infinity through the deaths of *coups de dés*, between the hazards of shipwrecks and the eternal circumstances of probable constellations.

A NECESSARY CAUTION

This gambling of the I is not necessarily a matter for jubilation but rather an effort to draw a promise (a constellation) out of wreckage. *Nothing will have taken place but the place*, to quote Mallarmé's poem once again, *except perhaps a constellation*. The celebrated fragmentation of the Cartesian subject [into "subject positions" and "author-subjects" "currently mobilized" by "predominant disciplinary mechanisms" (Butler 1990, p. xiii)] apparently puts an end to the violence establishing the unitary self; it begins, after all, as the violence of a new technological order demanding the partition of the subject into incommunicable functions. Schiller saw a problem here that is perhaps worth remembering again: if the unitary subject is a historical phenomenon (and, in this sense, a "fiction"), so is its contemporary decentering. The destruction of the Cartesian I, in and for itself, is thus hardly a lucky strike at the truth of the subject or a guarantee of the preclusion of Aldous Huxley's brave new world. Hence there is a certain ambiguity in Kristeva's position: on the one hand, there is the positive potential in the unsettling of the subject that resists closure; on the other hand, however, there is the collapse of Occidental psychic space with its disturbing consequences. Kristeva's aesthetization of the subject comes from the summoning of the fragmented self into the prospect of a ludic freedom, a freedom with rules, that is, one that resists both the unquestioning mode of technological utility and the allures of final answers.

Yet this summoning is problematic, as Kristeva's work has demonstrated with increasing acuteness. The effort to bestow utopian aesthetic life on fragmentation evokes Benjamin's (1977) reflections on the baroque as the expectation of a miracle out of the piling up of fragments, and on allegory as the life of irresistible decay and the form that finds its perfection in ruin. Such life is like the life of a corpse with its nails, that is, its deadness, growing. And yet Benjamin's allegory, this grim version of Schiller's sentimentality, is not entirely devoid of hope for, Benjamin asserts, "On the second part of its wide arc [allegorical reflection] returns, to redeem" (p. 232). The baroque redemption through the ruin-as-form thus implies that "a worldview can only be a worldview if it attempts to redeem a prior worldview. . . . This means that the being of the new worldview unfolds as a form of living through the death of the former worldview" (Angelova 1992).

The aesthetization of the subject as an answer to irresistible fragmentation might be regarded, consequently, as an attempt at rescuing the moribund worldview of the artist. In its polytopia, Kristeva's subject lives the ruin of the Cartesian ego; in its aesthetic playfulness, it inhabits the destruction of the artist and, beyond it, of the aristocratic ideal that refused to separate profession from life, work from play, and the private from the public. In this sense, Kristeva's ludic subject traces Benjamin's paradoxical arc of redemption and, like the ruin-as-form, "is bound to a twofold function of dying-as-living" (Angelova 1992). To put it briefly, it is allegorical.

So is transference love, the new love story that becomes part of Kristeva's agenda as the equivocal savior of courtly and romantic loves. Kristeva's treatment of transference love is emblematic of the efforts of utopia to conjure the principle of hope from the life of ruins (the growing nails of the corpse). Love, one remembers, is Schiller's perfect example of the deployment of aesthetic playfulness as opposed to the one-sided gravity of instinct and respect. Yet the whole of Kristeva's project involves a paradox insofar as it relies on a furthering of seriousness that has turned love (as distinct from sex) into a profession. Analytic love is paid love that offers conversation and understanding as the new commodity. Hence it is hardly surprising that "unlike Freud's patients, the [modern] borderline speaks of Eros and dreams of Agape" (Kristeva 1987b, p. 50). The analysand pays in order to be listened to—and loved. To be loved fairly and lucidly. "I love you, neither do I" (Kristeva 1987b, p. 12). The utopian perspective that runs through Kristeva's theory thus invariably has to be thought as precariously unglued from its questionable reverse, the way the polytopic subject is detached as the playfully liberated double of *homo laborans*, or the way transference love is detached from analytic reality as the new love story. What makes utopia thinkable in these circumstances is the excess that Schiller evokes as the source and hope of all playfulness—an excess, however, that is yoked to its dying. Utopia, as Kristeva (1991) inconclusively concludes, is a means, not an end. It makes sense only in conjunction with the world of its decay.

L'ÉTRANGÈRE ABOLIE

According to our translinguistic reading of Kristeva's *Revolution in Poetic Language*, the confident *n'abolira* ("will not abolish") that follows in Mallarmé's poem immediately after *folie*, inscribes the certainty of a polyhedral dice-I— that it cannot be abolished but only confirmed through gambling. This is the certainty that the mother will always be with us, singing and rejoicing in language (as an imaginary father). This certainty—a negation of loss— accompanies our consent to a constitutive exile and to a homeless life of meanings. "'I have lost an essential object that happens to be, in the final analysis, my mother,' is what the speaking being seems to be saying. 'But no, I have found her again in signs, or rather since I consent to lose her

I have not lost her (that is the negation), I can recover her in language'"
(Kristeva 1989, p. 43). Melancholy begins with the disavowal of this negation: "I have not not [sic!] lost her, she cannot be recovered, words are
of no avail." On the far side of the melancholy collapse of meaning, however, a certain perplexity occurs. We might describe it as the gambling away
of negation. "Have I lost something? I do not recall."[4]

The word *abolie* used by Mallarmé appears once again in similar circumstances in Kristeva's writing. As in the case with *Un Coup de Dés*, the
word occurs in a poem quoted by Kristeva (1989) in its entirety in a piv-
otal section of her book: the poem is Nerval's "*El Desdichado*" and the book,
Black Sun. That is, the situation is, as described earlier, a situation of mirroring and redoubling between the theoretician and her brother-poet.
Nerval's use of the word, however, is different from Mallarmé's.

This use has its own literary history involving both Nerval and
Mallarmé. According to a study of Nerval's *El Desdichado*, the hypnotic
alliterative combination in which he employs the word made the word
fashionable, which explains why Mallarmé turned to it six times in his
poetry (Kristeva 1989). Mallarmé is evoked in Kristeva's discussion as
the inheritor of *El Desdichado's* (the disinherited one, as we noted earlier) rare and musically compelling word. Within Kristeva's writing,
however, it is Nerval's use of the word that, interpreted as part of an anagram of his nostalgic longing for the lost territory, is superinscribed over
Mallarmé's.

Although it is a word employed by Mallarmé, not by Nerval, *folie*
(translated as "madness" in the English text) is brought forth by Kristeva
(1989) in her discussion of the *folie* of Nerval's poem. This time the folly,
however, is inflicted with the pain of an imaginary memory. It has a different scope that tells on the form and circumstances of *abolir*. Where in
Mallarmé, the word is negative (*n'abolira*), in Nerval it is positive (*abolie*);
in Mallarmé, the word is a verb in the future, while in Nerval it is a past
participle; in Mallarmé, the word is preceded by *folie*, while in Nerval it
is rhymed with *mélancolie*. *N'abolira* is now *abolie*; will not abolish has
become abolished; what is negated in the future has turned into an accomplished fact of the past; the constellations of chance have crumbled
into the ruined towers of loss; the daring and incestuously blissful *hasard*
(*az-zar*, *az-zahr*, I-dice, gambling) of the subject-in-process has meta-

---

4. This phenomenon is discussed in Green (1993).

morphosed into the suicide-bound theatre of El Desdichado (the dead, "unbreathing" one—bezdichanen in Bulgarian); and folly is exposed as melancholy.

As pain, in a word. Abolie—a-boli—боли—but it hurts. In Bulgarian, the mellifluous French past participle coincides acoustically with the very present and verbal meaning of pain—pain without specified origin, without subject or object. This double-tongued string of sounds with its convoluted gambling history, speaking simultaneously the abolished past and the unabolishable pain that accompanies it, is a little parable, all too neat perhaps, of the ways in which the mother tongue inscribes its transversal messages. Yet in the simple simultaneity of its doubleness, which deletes the hidden language through the very word for abolition, there is also a warning. The warning that the mother tongue, the pain of loss and, with all this, the strange, hidden face of Narcissus from where the tears come, can also, after all, disappear. That a боли may be aboli. At the far end of the inverted search for the mother, of the movement that loses her through the very effort to retrieve her, at the far end, that is, of the march toward other languages and metalanguages that has to compensate us for the constitutive matricide—at the very edge of these strategies, the successful matricide emerges as the unbreathing wielder of a dead mastery over languages. The machine, in a word. Or, as Kristeva has chosen to designate it, the polyglot.

TOTAL LANGUAGES, INCOMMENSURATE LANGUAGES

The book of Babel, according to Jorge Borges's "Library of Babel," can be read according to n number of different codes and yields each time a totally different but always meaningful message. The Babylonian book is an extreme illustration of Ferdinand de Saussure's arbitrariness of the sign. It opens its pages in monadic worlds that are impervious to each other but nevertheless converge in their mysteriously identical scripts. The Babylonian book projects its inalterable material substratum into the universes of different languages, signifying different things. A librarian's parable of how we share a language, it exposes the spectral craft of interpretation and embodies the mathematician's trust in isomorphism and anticipated meanings. "You who read me, are you sure you understand my language?" (Borges 1985, p. 79), asks the librarian. For even if we share a game, who can confirm that it is one and the same game we are playing?

If the Babylonian book were opened, however, by the savage from Knecht's poem "Alphabets" (in Herman Hesse's novel *The Glass Bead Game* (1943) to quote an ambitious modernist monster as against the sly post-modern maneuvering), what happens is not this or that meaning. The letters jump from the pages and display such a profusion of dangerous vitality that the terrified savage—quite ignorant of the reader's or the mathematician's games and it is precisely this ludic ineptitude that defines him as a "savage" here—sets the book on fire.

The burning reunites the dispersal of meanings, fuses the *n* number of codes in the flames. On the far end, this dispersal is assembled in the vision of a total language. In Hesse's *The Glass Bead Game*, the life of Knecht offered by his anonymous biographer is followed by three lives written by Knecht. These three lives function as alternative autobiographies of Knecht. His life *a fortiori* becomes for his biographer what the novel as a whole becomes for its author: an exercise of the same order as the writing of the lives ascribed to Knecht, that is, an exercise in inhabiting other places, times, and I-s. *The Glass Bead Game* players are, from this point of view, I-dice players; they regard the cultural field in its entirety as a reservoir for the assumption of multiple biographies.

Not without a price, however. *The Glass Bead Game* players' bookish reincarnations are carried out in the spirit of reverential disappearance into an authoritative figure. The game, situated beyond the memory of loss, demands the relinquishing of all artistic productivity. No creativity—no nature, no bodies, no women, to be sure—have place in this game. What is ludic about it, other than its sparkling uselessness, is the very preservation of a stern, stiffly hierarchical, ascetic authority that can no longer find its legitimacy in a beyond but has to rely on the players' self-sufficient drive for playing, *der Spieltrieb*. The players are hence playing at being mother-less and at having only a father who subjects them to his unmitigated and relentless rules; they are playing, in a word, although not without diffi-culty, at not being creative.

This extreme sternness is dictated by Hesse's solution to the problems of polyglottism. *The Glass Bead Game* realizes Humboldt's ideal of a total language that can bring all language games into a single game. A transpar-ent tower of Babel, the game requires utter submission from the phratry of its humble players. This inflexible strictness ensures the totalizing move-ment of the game; anything corporeal, creative and rebellious, anything semiotic, anything pertaining to the feminine, would unsettle its shared unified meaning.

The disembodiedness of Hesse's players demonstrates that the total language is opposed not only to the "recognition of the heteromorphous nature of language games" (Lyotard 1984, p. 66), to the realms of local narratives. It is opposed also to the savage's dangerously jumping letters or, to put it more precisely, it leaves behind the enigma of the body of the polyglot.

THE BODY OF THE POLYGLOT

A forgetful, anesthetized *El Desdichado*, the polyglot exemplifies the autonomy of the mask: its artificiality frozen beyond any playful recall. If the destiny of the speaking being is to be motherless—if matricide is the necessary condition for the advent of the subject—the polyglot offers the futility of perfection. The polyglot is, consequently, the one who has effectively lost the mother, the one who testifies to the very possibility of a loss without residue.

Being quite motherless, the polyglot has no body. He is like Borges's Babylonian book: he stands as the cipher of a disparate multiplicity of languages, demonstrating Saussure's dictum of the arbitrariness of the sign. The polyglot, one might say, is the very sign of this arbitrariness. Kristeva doubts Jakobson's famous statement that he speaks Russian in fifteen languages: this presence of the mother tongue as the entelechy behind the polyglottic versatility is, according to Kristeva, always problematic. If I am who *je suis*, my body will be dispersed across the multiple phonetic scales: the "narrative unity" that Seyla Benhabib (1992, p. 5) evokes as establishing the identity of the self is not sufficient to embody the subject. The question is, What makes a narrative unity (or a narrative fragmentation, for that matter) *mine*? Vis-à-vis the narrative, the body is precisely in the untranslatable connections that challenge the arbitrariness of the sign: I have a body if the language in which I say "I" has a body for me. Hence, insofar as it exists for me, the body is either a language-as-negation-of-loss (a phallic mother, an imaginary father)—a redoubling, from the very start, in which another body grows from within mine to embrace it and confirm its being—or it is a void, a startled blankness ("Have I lost something?").

It is not a total language that polyglottism requires but a body. This becomes apparent even in *The Glass Bead Game* where the search for a total language takes us finally to the young naked body of Tito. To Lacan's myth of the leap in the mirror, to Kristeva's myth of the leap of semiotic motility into language, the polyglot adds her parable of the mask demanding embodiment: a reversal of the parable of the mother lost through her being recovered. Now it is the flight from the mother that, successful at last, reveals her on the very horizon of meaning as the hope for a new incarnation.

UTOPIAN PROCEDURE 1: THE TRANSLINGUISTIC REGISTER

The hope is in a body, the body of the polyglot, piled up from the undefeatable meaning of fragments (Benjamin 1977). Amidst laughter and crying, this body erupts from the translinguistic register—the semiotic of the polyglot. There languages fuse and exchange energies. They merge and clash in the simultaneous transfigurations of orthography, sound, and rhythm, in the risk, the hazard, *le hasard*, the *az-zahr* of an alchemic transmutation.

UTOPIAN PROCEDURE 2: *TAT TVAM ASI*

If in Lacan's mirror stage I find myself as other in the image handed over to me, Kristeva repeats the question, How, then, do I find the other? and answers I find the other in the stranger that I, consequently, am bound to remain. If I am other, the stranger is myself. Through this *tat tvam asi* detour, I am the other and the other is me only to the extent that we are strangers to ourselves—to the extent that we do not reduce strangeness and our constitutive exile. Communication—and community—is a recognition of, and lucidity about, strangeness. Even if language games are irreducibly heteromorphous, what cannot be spoken delineates our common horizon. Kristeva inquires into strangeness as precisely the thing that we share with others. Strangeness becomes a universal feature and the cornerstone of universality in a (utopian) world without boundaries. Asymbolia and the feminine are revealed as that residue of universal strangeness whose recognition will make possible the tolerance of "multiple logics, speeches and existences" (Kristeva 1977, p. 9).

LANGUAGE AND NAÏVETÉ

It is at the dawn of a new polyglottic and cosmopolitan world that the murderous children of Clytemnestra, absolved by Aeschylus, rendered seamlessly righteous by Sophocles, return, with Euripides, to take another look at the mother's corpse. What they find out is that Apollo, who urged them to commit the murder and who, consequently, sang of dim justice but inflicted upon them an obvious evil, can no longer serve effectively his traditional function of purging the shedding of blood. He himself, with his senseless and uproarious speeches, shares the guilt. Once its senseless brutality is laid bare, purging—bestowing meaning on horror—can no longer be effected through the Apollonian jurisdiction. At the limits of polyglottism, allegory returns to demand a new meaning on the far side of the mother's death.

With the uncertainty of justice and the clarity of evil at hand, Kristeva's (1980) polylogue offers its wager not of absolute truth, but of "a little more truth" (p. ix). The speaking being is constituted as an exile in language, yet from this perspective of strangeness, from an expositioning with regard to meaning, emerges the utopia of a world without boundaries, a world that is constituted as a polyglottic community of strangers, an exile from language, in the translinguistic trajectory toward the body. Revisiting Schiller's paradox, could we state that if language has been so much at the center of last century's discussions, it is because we have lost our naive unity with it? The naive poet—and this is something Schiller realized—is at one with nature; but this instantly and immediately means that he is at one with language, that he is the human-being-as-language. With our second separation, the one that makes us avid scholars of language the way Schiller's contemporaries were passionate lovers of nature, Kristeva's polyglot emerges as the epitome of a new species, a mistress of languages that is never in them. Sentimentality becomes a longing for language [not desire "in" as in Kristeva's Desire in Language (1980) but desire "for" as in her preface to the book]. It becomes a longing for the naïveté that speaks. Catapulted from the father's head into the open spaces of Urania, is it another Schillerian infinity that we have to draw before a reunion is foreseen—a reunion with the naïveté that speaks rather than speak its longing for speaking? The reunion has to be foreseen outside of its forever returning wide arc.

The polylogue offers a genre for the theory conscious of its passions. With Kristeva, it describes a parabolic movement in which the theoretical quest for an irretrievable object is approached, like Plato's chora, only through difficult reasoning. The quest returns as the narrative of a flight from that object. Defying Oedipus's fate, the polylogue tries to go back home, but the paradoxical geometry of its wandering destines it to find itself further and further away from home, always under foreign skies. Oedipus's universe consists of one point; however desperately he may try to move from that point and unfold it into a path, he remains fixed under the single ray of his fate. The polylogue multiplies spaces through its very effort to reach the unique source of invisible light. The polylogue thus exemplifies the condition of the modern speaking being. Oedipus is given a fate that dictates the one-point geometry of his universe. The modern speaking being is offered the geometry of proliferating spaces and this is her destiny.

According to Kristeva, these spaces, if they are to challenge the closure of meaning, have to be given as new ways of speaking. In this sense the unfolding spaces of the polylogue are polyglottic: they propagate through the translation of a secret and irrecoverable Ur-text. Along this parabola, the parabola of indefatigable translation, the polylogue reverses the segregation of the disciplines and the breaking up of genres, and, in an apparent movement toward their fusion, holds all the strings of this prodigious instrument that is language. It plunges into the translinguistic register, into the baroque body of the polyglot.

Yet it does not remain there. Due to a knowledge effect attributed by Kristeva to psychoanalytic discourse, the polylogue preserves the distinctness of its voices. It enacts the drama of wandering as a wandering through languages and disciplines.

The polylogue, hence, is a parable—a parabola—of exile. A double exile: the father is the symbolic function that separates from the archaic mother of primordial union, but the ensuing disconsolate quest for the lost territory constitutes the speaking being as a perennial foreigner to the symbolic. The polylogue uncovers the impossibility of a naive unity with language and unfolds the trajectory of a new sentimental infinity.

An exile who asks "Where?", a restless wanderer obsessed with drawing boundaries and dividing spaces, the polylogue is the genre of Kristeva's subject-in-process absorbed in its play of self-creation and rebirth. It is in rebirth, in the coincidence of renovation with the corroded memory, that the polylogue retrieves its specific temporality. The ludic subject is hence revealed as baroque in Benjamin's sense: it finds its form in the ruin of the figure of the artist. In a perennially belated epoch, this ludic subject, the agent of a forever dwindling revolution, has as its life the decay of artistic creativity, and in this sense is the murderous redeemer of the utopia of aesthetic education. The mother reappears in the distance of longing and critique.

Part II

The Lineage of Silence

4

The Abjective Stance

Why, what spur is there so keen as to drive to matricide?
Aeschylus, The Eumenides

In "Fantasy Echo," Joan Scott (2001) delineates, on the basis of feminist movements, two fantasy scenarios: there is, on the one hand, the orator, a solitary woman standing at a podium, addressing a male audience and experiencing her speaking as a transgressive jouissance; there is, on the other hand, the "utopian fantasy of sameness and harmony produced by maternal love" (p. 293). On the basis of these coextensive fantasies, repetitively and inadvertently enacted throughout the history of feminist movements, Scott elaborates the concept of "fantasy echo" as a model for identity constructions that "elide historical differences and create apparent continuities" (p. 304). For Scott, such a misleading identity produced by the elision of historical differences and the creation of apparent continuities is "woman." My argument reverses hers in order to emphasize the circularity of the phenomenon. It is not that these two fantasies produce the false identity "woman"; rather, it is "woman" that functions as the fantastic oscillation between radical discontinuity and seamless continuity, suspending the unfolding of a historical narrative in both cases. Seen synchronically, this diachronic oscillation takes the form of an oscillation between fusion and abjection. It is largely responsible for the fragility and instability of the feminist discursive field and for its chronically embattled status.

I will designate the rhetorical ramifications of abjection and fusion as "abjectivity" and "merginality" (with an "e"). I discuss merginality in Chapter 5. Unlike merginality, which has its pleasurable extras, abjectivity is a rather bleak theoretical task that, furthermore, induces its reenactment. Abjectivity is literary assassination. Objective—subjective—abjective. The woman author is, to use a term that Margaret Ferguson (1985) takes out of *Hamlet*, "incorpsed" and thrown out of the body proper of literature. "The letter killeth," is Ferguson's quotation, most pertinent for the case at hand (p. 292). Abjectivity is a radically antihermeneutic procedure that demands sentence first and verdict afterward, extracting dead bodies rather than meanings. The murder-through-letter is carried out as a blatant inattentiveness toward the texts of the incorpsed author and yet, careless as it is about words, abjectivity cannot be reduced to a simple scholarly negligence. It is bent on the reading of a more difficult text, a transcendent text where, on the far side of words, a faulty and culpable female body, as is the case with the frigid childless body of Woolf, is exposed before being abjected.

JOYCE'S SISTER

In an attempt to overcome the embarrassment of feminist misconstruals of Virginia Woolf, Toril Moi (1985) suggests in *Sexual/Textual Politics* that Woolf should be read via Julia Kristeva. Moi indicates certain directions for a Kristevan interpretation, focusing on Woolf's treatment of gender identity. At the time, however, Kristeva's own suggestion for reading Woolf was the following one:

> In women's writing, language seems to be seen from a foreign land; is it seen from the point of view of an asymbolic, spastic body? Virginia Woolf describes suspended states, subtle sensations and, above all, colours— green, blue—, but she does not dissect language as Joyce does. Estranged from language, women are visionaries, dancers who suffer as they speak. [Kristeva 1981, p. 166]

Although dating back to 1974, to a time when many of Kristeva's books were yet unwritten, this statement about Woolf, far from being an ad hoc illustration, prefigures much of Kristeva's later theory. Estranged from language, seeing it from afar, painfully envisioning it from the foreign land of an asymbolic body, Woolf's location anticipates the topology elaborated in Kristeva's subsequent theoretical works: a topology that specifies the speaking being's relation to language in terms of exile, nostalgia, and empty distances. As already discussed, the "as if" attitude to the social and symbolic order of the feminine brings about a disequilibrium that may result in overzealous identification with this order ("I am not this but I can play the game and I can play it better than others"), or to a melancholic crumbling down. Insofar as she "suffers as she speaks," Woolf is drawn toward the shadowy space of what Kristeva (1989) termed "the hidden face of my philosophy, her mute sister" (p. 14): the space of melancholy, of thwarted enunciation, of speechlessness, and suicidal stasis. And yet the risks that the feminine positioning with respect to language entails, are accompanied by the potential for renewal and revolt and allow the distance of critique, of the "eternal irony of the community." It is by inhabiting the split, rather than wavering to the one or the other side, that this potential is uncovered. From this point of view, Woolf's foreignness to language places her in the category of the singular achievements of the female geniuses that Kristeva studies in her latest work and—to use Joan Scott's term—echoes Kristeva's own constitutive foreignness.

Nevertheless, it is noteworthy that in this Kristevan passage Woolf is opposed to Joyce, who was frequently celebrated as the great example *of écriture feminine*. In her own epoch, although she was not spared abjective criticism, Woolf was perceived as representative of the innovative trends of her age. In *Mimesis*, Erich Auerbach (1948) chose to make her the representative novelist for the first half of the twentieth century. By the end of the twentieth century, in spite of the continuously growing archives dedicated to her, Woolf had definitely lost this position, while Joyce's centrality was enhanced by, among other things, his status as a champion of femininity. The feminine Joyce and the asymbolic Woolf thus come very close to the coupling that Woolf delineates in *A Room of One's Own* between the androgynous Shakespeare and Shakespeare's sister who gets drowned without leaving a literary legacy. I will call "abjective" the reading that, from the split characterizing the feminine—the split between an asymbolic body and a distant and ironic dwelling in language ripe with the potential for rebellion and critique—produces only the body. Preferably dead. Shakespeare's sister.

THE ANGEL IN THE HOUSE

In the 1970s Elaine Showalter launched a critique on Woolf in a book whose title, *A Literature of Their Own*, sounds like a modification of one of Woolf's famous titles, but that, as Showalter (1999) insists in a new expanded edition of her book, refers in fact to John Stuart Mill. For Kristeva, Woolf, a dancer and a visionary, is estranged from language. The estrangement springs from a spastic body to which the phallic order offers no symbolization. For Showalter, Woolf is estranged from her body. She is separated from corporeal experience because of her frigidity and childlessness. Evading the fact that her anguish comes from the crises connected with menstruation or menopause (Showalter 1977), Woolf deprived herself of female experience and remained bound by her "female aestheticism." Because Woolf forsook her body, expression failed her and she committed a "betrayal of her literary genius" (Showalter 1977, p. 264).

Showalter (1977) demands the killing of "the Angel in the house, that phantom of female perfection who stands in the way of freedom and who turns out to be Woolf herself" (p. 265). Yet it was Woolf who, in "Professions for Women" (1942, pp. 149–154), took pride in having killed the Angel in the house. She killed her by throwing an inkpot at her: a gesture referring to Martin Luther's acclaimed attack on the devil, and implying that the Angel in the house is the woman-writer's devil. At the same time, if the deadly weapon is an inkpot, it is because this adversary is the Angel of silence, the opponent of writing, the mute double. The silent doubles's murder by inkpot is thus "part of the occupation of a woman writer" (Woolf 1942, p. 151). This coincides with the woman writer's coming into being: "Had I not killed her, she would have killed me. She would have plucked the heart out of my writing" (p. 51). Plucking the heart out of my writing, she would have killed me; the heart of my writing is my heart; I am my writing and I am writing through vanquishing my silent double, the metaphysical adversary of speech.

The feminine split is resolved through a murder that secures the place of the subject on the side of language. Woolf's combat with the Angel of silence is not that innocent: she did have an ambiguous inclination to examine her foremothers in the context of tombs and mausoleums concentrating on their bodies rather than their books (Gilbert and Gubar 1988). Ironically, Woolf's victory over the Angel of silence is remembered (repeated) by Showalter at the price of positioning Woolf herself in the place of the moribund Angel. Woolf spoke through killing the Angel. Showalter speaks through killing Woolf. Woolf's deadly displacement to the position of her own Angel, this belated efficiency of her antagonist, is carried out, as Showalter (1977) terms it, through borrowing Woolf's "own murderous imagery" (p. 265). Through the borrowing of this imagery, Woolf coincides with the threatening double whom she believed she overcame: what is borrowed from Woolf is her own murder, which dislocates her from the speaking position to the position of her dead adversary.

In fact, the killing is somewhat redundant for, according to Showalter (1977), Woolf's writing is a suicide, a sort of self-immolation: her concept of androgyny is "an embrace of death" (p. 280), her "female aesthetic is . . . receptivity to the point of self-destruction" (p. 296) and her "vision of womanhood is as deadly as it is disembodied. The ultimate room of one's own is the grave" (p. 297). Unlike Woolf's Angel, who is said to have died hard, Showalter's Angel (Woolf) seems to be, anyway, already dead. Showalter is killing a corpse, killing it, moreover, through a ricochet of the corpse's own weapon. Speaking about Woolf's "ambiguity of violence" (p. 264), Showalter in the same breath lines her own violent act with the ambiguous justification that it is directed toward a victim of self-destruction. She is trampling a dead body. This is a movement that destroys a self-destroyed killer, a movement that only "borrows" an already committed murder, a movement of perfect circularity in which Woolf is threatened to be killed by the Angel, kills the Angel, threatens to kill as the Angel, is killed as the Angel, is therefore killed by the Angel (as in a science-fiction nightmare of time travel, where one moves back and forth in time only to meet one's proliferating doubles in an endless round of self-engendering and self-annihilation). Should we add that in this circle, Showalter, by killing Woolf the Angel, is playing Woolf's Angel?

"I look for myself throughout the centuries and I don't see myself anywhere," asserts Cixous (1975, p. 75). But, she adds, "if my desire is possible, it means the system is already letting something else through" (p. 78). Is it, indeed? Following Cixous, who stated this in 1975, we might ask how many times this finally granted possibility of "my desire" has been repeated? How many times has the system let something else through just for me? In her introduction to *The Newly Born Woman*, Sandra Gilbert (1986) notes that Cixous's reiteration of points made earlier in England and America seems almost "uncanny" (p. xvi). And yet, Cixous's uncanny reiteration seems to be reiterating points made earlier, also in France. For example, when the first edition of *The Second Sex* appeared in 1949, Simone de Beauvoir wrote and by her very theoretical stance exemplified that women "have no past, no history" (p. xix). On the other hand, as Gilbert's own examples illustrate, as in the above-mentioned introduction but also throughout the bulk of her research, this uncanniness applies to the English and American authors as well. Before Virginia Woolf asked in the early twentieth century why there wasn't a tradition of the mothers, Elizabeth Barrett Browning sadly noted, around the middle of the nineteenth century, that "I look everywhere for grandmothers and find none" (quoted in Gilbert 1986, p. xvi). At the beginning of the nineteenth century the recurring proclamation of generic loneliness is voiced by the uncanny itself: "When I looked around, I saw and heard of none like me" (Shelley 1818, p. 120). Mary Shelley's motherless Monster, a unique and disconsolate murderer, sprung from the imagination of a daughter whose birth literally killed her mother. It seems to echo the words of this very mother, no other woman but Mary Wollstonecraft (1979), the acknowledged mother of feminism, who in 1787 described herself as being "the first of a new genus" (p. 164).

Gilbert and Gubar's monumental work on women's literary history constantly brings in evidence about the matricidal phantasmatic with its offspring of unique voices. The reason why Gilbert and Gubar do not single out the point where their uncanny examples crystallize is that, of course, their work is part of the huge collective effort in the recent decades to recuperate the missing mother—recuperate her, so to say, with all the missing parts: the everything of the mother. In its ultimate effects, this recuperation is "merginal" and takes us to a disturbing fact that Brenda Silver (1989) pointed out in connection with Woolf: the fact that this type of recuperation has had very little effect on the public sphere and that between 1938 and the end of the 1990s "little if anything had changed in this respect" (p. 221).

Why isn't there a tradition of the mothers? Woolf turns to look back in the literary past and, in spite of her own writing on so many female predecessors, sees no literary mothers. She sees "strange spaces of silence" separating the solitary female utterances throughout history (Woolf 1958, p. 77). Far from offering an escape from the "infernal repetition," as Cixous hopes, writing tends to reproduce the figure of the missing mother. The Angel is killed and killed, the silence is enunciated and enunciated, generating Angels and silence.

MATRICIDE

What makes the transposition of Woolf into an Angel of silence so striking is the circularity that this transposition involves. Both Shakespeare's sister and the Angel of the house are Woolf's allegories of female silence. By her referral to their place, Woolf (didn't this frigid suicidal woman drown herself as Shakespeare's sister did?) is turned into an allegory of silence and, as we shall presently see, into an archetype. Thus Woolf's concern with the tradition of the mothers, according to Showalter (1977), did not get her anywhere, because "by the end of her life she had gone back full circle, back to the melancholy, guilt-ridden, suicidal women—Lady Winchelsea and the Duchess of Newcastle—whom she had studied and pitied" (p. 264). The Duchess of Newcastle, as Woolf commented, produced "quartos and folios that nobody ever reads" (Woolf 1935, p. 92). Going back is the circular gesture that puts Woolf's own writing on the shelf of those unreadable quartos and folios. Woolf goes back, she makes a full circle, her enunciation of the lack of a tradition of the mothers adds to this lack, to this tradition of lack. Woolf is the Duchess of Newcastle is Shakespeare's sister is the Angel of the house is silence is . . .

Madness, after all. Showalter privileges Woolf's diary (or her manuscripts) as the authentic place where the real Woolf can be found, while the texts she chose to present to the world are seen as the crippled result of compromise and self-betrayal. Woolf's anger becomes one of the topoi of this diary-based authenticity: the real Woolf, as indicated by her diary, was angry; the Woolf who believed, for whatever reason, that "the temptation to anger" (Woolf 1958, p. 80) should be resisted, was the product of a secondary and reductive state.[1] A hierarchy of genres is thus established, at the top of which is, as reputedly the most angry, the diary; the rest of Woolf's writing is regarded as the obscuring deformation of this primal source. But why is a diary more authentic than a novel or an essay? Why is anger more authentic than the impulse to win your audience by controlling your anger? In Woolf's case such privileging disregards her quite conscious strategies for beating the system and questions the very possibility (then and there) of a deliberation that does not amount to conformity. It is

---

1. Among the important proponents of this view is Adrienne Rich (1979), who "was astonished at the sense of effort, of pains taken, of dogged tentativeness" (p. 37) in the tone of *A Room of One's Own*.

hardly surprising that the search for the authentic goes finally beyond the diary, which, however spontaneous, still has the setback of being mediated through writing. Madness is now Woolf's clearest articulation: madness was the role in which she articulated her resentment and rage (Showalter 1977).

One could presume, of course, that madness is a timeless artistic privilege, that poetic inspiration has always been regarded as equivocally close to insanity. Plato wrote about the divine madness of poets and distinguished it, in Phaedrus, from the left-handed madness due to human sicknesses. In the history of the new European literatures the insanity of Torquato Tasso turned him into the paradigmatic poet. Montaigne (1948) referred to him as the example of the proximity of genius and derangement in the countless minds that "have been ruined by their very power and suppleness" (p. 363). Goethe, who believed that a poet should have a "very delicate organization" in order to hear "celestial voices" (Eckermann 1930, p. 335), wrote a drama about Tasso. Schopenhauer (1819) offered a discussion of this view, quoting, among others, Alexander Pope as saying "great wits to madness sure are near allied" (p. 191). The myth was fervently exemplified by the romantics: Hölderlin spent half of his long life in a blackout. The even more famous breakdown of Nietzsche followed. Still closer to Woolf, Marcel Proust noted that "one of the characteristic features of our times is that its wise men are more or less mad" (quoted in Kristeva 1994, p. 131, n. 5) and Thomas Mann developed his theory of the sick genius of the aristocrats of the spirit (Nietzsche, Dostoevsky) and the healthy genius of the aristocrats of nature (Goethe, Tolstoy). In a recent account of an imaginary encounter between Woolf and Foucault, Michèle Barrett (1999) almost dares to say that the influence of Foucault is due to his role of the fool who dares say his insane truth.

In a manner analogous to Plato's dichotomy of the divine and the left-handed madness, however, two paradigms are involved in the discussion of Woolf's madness: one is the paradigm of the mad artist who, on the far side of madness, hears "celestial voices"; the other is the paradigm of the mad woman, who, whatever she hears, is heard only by her doctor. King Lear is mad and wise; Hamlet is mad (may be) and outstanding; Ophelia is mad and pitiful. The significance of the artist is beyond his insanity, insanity being only the dire recompense for the artist's outstanding imprint on history; the mad woman is imprisoned in her insanity, locked in a timeless limbo without exit. While authors like Gilbert and Gubar see their task in the rehabilitation of the madwoman in the attic; while Jean Rhys does this by turning to Rochester's first mad wife, thus giving voice to the unwritten narrative behind Jane Eyre, the question is why Showalter sends the writer Woolf to the attic? Why is Woolf relegated to the "left-handed" madness and not to the madness of poets? Why should Woolf's madness be interpreted as her true medium of expression rather than, as Moi (1985) timidly suggests, as the price for artistic excellence, for the risks arising from the disruption of the symbolic order? Why, in other words, should Showalter (1977) take arms so passionately against the idea of Woolf's "divine seizure by the muse" (p. 267)? In spite of her novels, Woolf ends up as "the real-life epitome of that feminine archetype, the Mad Wife" (p. 276). She is taken out of her own writing and thrown into an archetype—and out of history.

Put into the terms of Kristeva's theory of matricide, Woolf is abjected. The role that bodily considerations play in Showalter's repudiation of Woolf is fascinating: Woolf's food preferences, sexual relations with Leonard, frigidity, childlessness, molestation by her brother, menstruation, and menopause, are discussed at great length along with—or rather instead of—the analysis of her writing and ideas. Woolf is reinterpreted as a body, not as an erotic body, to be sure, but as a compendium of malfunctions, as the body of medicine and physiology. Showalter criticizes Woolf for having rejected her malfunctioning body and, so to say, returns this body to her—turns her into this body, before rejecting her as this body. What a faulty body Woolf had! Let us impose on her this faulty body whose secrets we will deliciously rummage, so that we can denounce the writer Woolf. Matricide, according to Kristeva, is precisely a rejection of the mother's body, of the mother as a body. It is subtended by the settling of accounts with the interior of the maternal body. Reinterpreting Woolf's writing into an asymbolic, spastic body and then throwing this body out of literary history, therefore, is an exemplification of such a maternal execution. Its mythically recurring character is emphasized by the borrowing of the murder, the murdering of the already murdered, the reversal of the victor into her own victim. Through the circularity that it exhibits, Showalter's murderous naïveté calls in question not simply Woolf's standing as a writer but, most of all, her lifelong concern with the tradition of the mothers. As Showalter asserts, this concern led Woolf back; it delineated a full circle, and Woolf ended as the hapless Duchess of Newcastle and the luckless Lady Winchilsea, whom Woolf (1935) quotes and whom, according to Showalter, Woolf finally joins:

For groves of laurel thou wert never meant;
Be dark enough thy shades, and be thou there content. [p. 89]

THE PARADOX OF THE LIBRARY

In Woolf's discussion of the tradition of the mothers, she is aware of the difficult and problematic nature of her project. Woolf formulates this difficulty in terms of a paradox that I will call the paradox of the library. Alternating scenes of different libraries in *A Room of One's Own* (the Oxbridge library, the British Museum, the private library with the shelves of the readable and the shelves of the unreadable, the bookcases of the dead and the bookcases of the living), Woolf outlines the impediments that barred women from entering the library: the lack of education, the lack of good education, and the interdictions enforced by beadles and guardian angels. But literature is open to everybody. "I refuse to allow you, Beadle though you are, to turn me off the grass" (Woolf 1935, p. 113).

It is the fraudulence of this openness that *A Room of One's Own* finally faces. All else said and done, it has to be realized that the British Museum is only "another department of the factory" (Woolf 1935, p. 39). Entering "under the vast dome, as if one were a thought in the huge bald forehead which is so splendidly encircled by a band of famous names" (p. 40), a woman discovers that she is a "somewhat harassed thought" (p. 44). The library, however spacious the bald forehead of its collective *nous* might seem, is not keen on thinking this thought. Granted at last the chance to be in the library, a woman reads there her exclusion from it.

A similar disappointment of the reader, betrayed in her hopes for finding support for her rebellion in the "antiland" of the library, emerges in Cixous (1986): "In my imaginary camp, aggressors appear; the friend is also the enemy" (pp. 74–75). Between the Angel of silence and the harassing library (a friend who is also an enemy), Woolf represents the specific difficulty that the symbolic order presents to the feminine. A woman has to either enter the seemingly open "antiland" of the library as a pure intelligence—that is, regard gender as generally dispensable—or encounter repeatedly the signs of her exclusion. In the spirit of the eternal irony of the community, I suggested in an earlier text that the flinging of the inkpot at the Angel of silence should be balanced by the method of flinging the book. The reader reads for some time, flings the book, thinks for some time, takes it back, thumps the dust off, reads again, flings it again (Nikolchina 1992). Woolf, however, was contemplating far darker temptations.

AN APPROACH THROUGH FIRE

There was one solution to the paradox of the library Woolf knew to be always open: fire. Woolf's frequent and emphatic references to fire, to the proximity of illumination and burning, give her cogitations a blazing frame. They form one of the most tenacious links between *A Room of One's Own* and the later *Three Guineas*, which is said by Woolf (1953) to have gathered "enough powder to blow up St. Paul's" (p. 175), and which offers its own sinister leitmotif of "Rags, Petrol, Matches" as the alternative to a compromise that cannot and yet has to be accepted. Fire indicates the silence of the past (Shakespeare's sister burns her scribblings); fire is the promise of the future (Mary Carmichael will eventually light the torch); the resisted and yet constantly suggested temptation of fire (the inimical apparition turned into a burning bush, the guinea given for rags, petrol, and matches) lines the present. Significantly, therefore, it is among the burning bushes, in a framework of fire and circuiting, so to say, via the ambiguity of fire, that, in *A Room of One's Own*, Mary Beton begins her wandering from one library into another. This imagery casts a bridge from the serene hope of *A Room of One's Own* to the radical utopia of *Three Guineas*, the utopia of "cheap, easily combustible material which does not hoard dust and perpetrate traditions" (Woolf 1938, p. 39).

The landscape at the beginning of *A Room of One's Own* is, in fact, more complicated. It includes the river reflecting "whatever it chose of sky and bridge and burning tree" (Woolf 1935, p. 8). All the elements of this landscape are transferred, but in a rather dramatic manner, to *Three Guineas*: the river, the burning, the open sky, the bridge that becomes the major metaphor for the divided situation of woman. In the later book these images are highly ambiguous, informed by the suspicion that we are presented with a "choice of evils. . . . Had we not better plunge off the bridge into the river; give up the game; declare that the whole of human life is a mistake and so end it?" (Woolf 1938, p. 86). Leaving aside the judgmental pathos against the "melancholy, guilt-ridden, suicidal women," we have to recognize the striking coincidence between Woolf's dilemma and the precarious split that Kristeva conceptualizes as the feminine. From within this split, Woolf's writing, like her life, was constantly resumed in a gesture of radical and ruthless questioning. Burning was one of the persistent metaphors for her readiness to carry out her inquiry to the end.

A book of wrath, gloomy and full of powder, created as it is in the shadow of the Second World War, *Three Guineas* seems to be the exact opposite of *A Room of One's Own* in all its important conceptual turns. *A Room of One's Own* offers a program firmly based on the values of writing (it is important that women should write books), permanence (there is a reality and a writer has the chance of facing it more often than other people), and fame (Shakespeare's future sister who will be born from our obscure efforts). *Three Guineas*, on the other hand, elaborates its much more disconcerting "virtues of obscurity" (Woolf 1938, p. 133): silence and evasion, secrecy and elasticity, and, above all, temporariness, an emphasis on the fragile and perishable "work of the living" (p. 39). Permanence versus combustibility, celebrity versus secrecy, writing versus silence, a preoccupation with tradition versus the "freedom from loyalty to old schools" (p. 90), androgyny as the sublime man-womanly fusion versus the utter split of the Outsiders Society in *Three Guineas*: far from differing only in their tone, in their resisting or yielding to anger, the two projects seem to embody the wavering of the feminine between the "as if" of playing the game and the "silent underwater body . . . abdicating any entry into history" (Kristeva 1981, p. 166). Death by drowning. And yet, however different Woolf's projects in those two books might seem, they converge in their fiery edges. Showalter's abjective criticism of Woolf's resistance to the "temptation to anger" overlooks the fact that, for Woolf, the alternative to this resistance is not putting anger to paper but the much more extreme attraction of burning. Of terrorism. Only against this radical background and only in conjunction with this radical background that gives a framework of flames to any tentative ("combustible") conclusion, can Woolf's ethics of writing and form acquire its precise profile.

THE TURN OF ANDROGYNY

In *A Room of One's Own*, the questions discussed before the issue of androgyny appears are mostly concerned with the tradition of the mothers: Why were our mothers so poor? which is the same question as Why didn't they write? and Is whatever they wrote—when they did at last—of the kind that we can continue? After the confrontation with the burning apparition in the British Museum, a certain chronology is followed throughout Beton's ramblings among the bookcases. It reaches the present time with Mary Carmichael and then goes on to androgyny, which is the last thing that Mary Beton has to say, the conclusion to her musings. This conclusion, however, seems to confound rather than to clarify the preceding discussion.

In fact, it contradicts the discussion that it is supposed to close. Through an unexpected movement, androgyny screens the poignancy of the preceding search for a tradition of the mothers, introducing its own contrasting story. If the first story is a story about the silence of Shakespeare's sister, the second story is about the (androgynous) eloquence of Shakespeare. The first story is a story about the absence of the mothers; the second one is about their presence, for "poetry ought to have a mother as well as a father" (Woolf 1935, p. 155). The first story insists that "it is useless to go to the great men writers for help" (p. 114); the second story affirms that "when I want to stretch my faculties on a book . . . [I] turn back to Shakespeare" (p. 156). The result is a bewildering reevaluation: the suicidal epoch when Shakespeare's sister killed herself one winter night in this second story is called "that happy age," for "Shakespeare was androgynous" (p. 156).

What seems to follow is that it is impossible to look simultaneously at the story of androgyny and at the story about the obscurity of the mother. The two stories tend to shroud each other, to conceal each other. Situated as it is on a turn—the turning back to Shakespeare—the story of androgyny finds its own specific landscape by turning away from the other landscape, the landscape of the absent mother. What story, what landscape you are looking at seems to be an outcome of the turning you have taken: a happy turn leads you to Mary Carmichael; a turning back leads you to androgyny; with Aphra Behn you "turn an important corner on the road" (Woolf 1935, p. 95); if you take the right turning you go from Oxbridge to Fernham.

It is, in the long run, the turn of fiction, for, we are warned at the beginning, *A Room of One's Own* cannot give us the truth about fiction (or woman). All it can give us is a fiction, the fiction about truth. Androgyny is a turn on this road with many corners and without closure. A fictional turn, to be sure, for having taken this turn with the fictional "I" of Mary Beton, we can then turn away both from androgyny and from Mary Beton (this is the last thing she has to say) and turn, "creatures of illusion as we are" (Woolf 1935, p. 52), through another fictional "I," the "I" of the framing story, back to Shakespeare's sister. Not to her dark past, however, but to her rebirth. Androgyny is a mediating temporary mask: it is something to help us read, perhaps to help us live. It is the turn from Shakespeare to his future sister.

THE MASK

Androgyny, therefore, is a fictional turn that is akin to the mask. To understand why this turn, the turn of androgyny, is at all necessary, one needs to remember the sorrowful revelation about the bald forehead of the library. In *A Room of One's Own*, androgyny facilitates a turn back to the library after the discovery that the woman's thought that enters the library is a somewhat harassed thought. Androgyny is the fictional turn—the "as if"—that allows the library to be entered but entered only provisionally, on certain conditions, under the sign of combustibility, with the rigor required by playing. In its function, it is analogous to Kristeva's use of the male mask: speaking via a male artist who speaks via a female double who further splits into a male/female couple (Nerval, who turns the name of Artemis in the masculine and then plays with the two members of the couple as if each were the double of the other); wearing the mask of a wearer of masks (Stendhal, with his love of seeming and masks, of pretenses and approximations); approaching the mother through the name of a man/the father, which is in fact the name of a woman/the mother (Céline is the writer's grandmother's name, while Nerval is an anagram of the poet's mother's name). This male masquerade is Kristeva's own masquerade in the enunciation of the great maternal passion, which turns out to be a passion for words, after all. The library with its wreath of famous names is transformed into a theatre where the I (*je*) is only insofar as it plays (*jeu*): from mask to mask, from one identity to another, and from language to language.

Through all these turns, the meaning, like the meaning of Greek in Woolf's (1925b) essay "On Not Knowing Greek," is just on the far side of language. In this essay, the allure of the "well-sunned nature, [of] the man who practices the art of living to the best advantage" and who makes us "seek truth with every part of us" (p. 52) is ultimately the allure of a language that cannot be known and that hints at the far more disconcerting Greek, which Septimus Smith from *Mrs. Dalloway* (Wolf 1925a) hears. Septimus Smith believes that the sparrows speak Greek. It also seems to him that the spaces between the birds' sounds are as significant as the sounds. In his hallucination Greek coincides with a birds' language in which the intervals are as significant as the sounds. This is a language singing in piercing Greek syllables from trees in the meadow of life where there is no crime and no death. It is only in her late work that Woolf, employing the significance of the spaces between the sounds, achieves a final—and breath-taking—solution to the problem of the murdered mother and the empty spaces through which she returns. What matters for the time being is the function of Greek as a metaphor for the maternal Ur-language, the impos-sible language that can drive us mad but that, also, drives us to seek truth with every part of us.

"On Not Knowing Greek" is not about not knowing Greek. It is about the impossibility of knowing Greek. As I already mentioned, Kristeva doubts Jakobson's confidence that he speaks Russian in fifteen languages. We try to speak the mother tongue in any language, in all languages. Yet we never speak the mother tongue itself, we never know Greek, the matrix of languages, the language from the meadows of life where there is no death, the language that can sing and vibrate in the clear spaces beyond air, beyond the neces-sity of mediation. Nevertheless, it is this language that, like the open, spare landscapes of Greek, "has us most in bondage; the desire for that which perpetually lures us back" (Woolf 1925b, p. 55). Back to the library.

BORN FROM THE HEAD

Athena is not very popular with interpreters who rightly see her as suspi-ciously uncontaminated by the womb (Spivak 1988), the epitome of the daughter without a mother, the type of the female upholder of patriarchy. Indeed, in Aeschylus's trilogy, Athena, being born from Zeus's head, stands as the witness for the dispensability of the mother, and her vote is decisive for the legitimation of matricide, a matricide and a legitimation so thor-ough, in fact, that the child is said to have one parent, a father only. With its bizarre conclusion, Aeschylus's trilogy offers a striking contrast to Sophocles's rendering of the great ancient myth of patricide: while patri-cide leads Oedipus, the murderer, into exile and transforms him by mak-ing him bend to the inscrutable will of the gods, matricide, on the contrary, is the promise for a return from exile for the murderer Orestes. Matricide has the extraordinary result of transforming the gods, more precisely cer-tain goddesses, the Erinyes, who are made to bend before the rulings of a human institution, the Areopagus of Athens. Matricide, as rendered by Aeschylus, becomes the vehicle for a modification of the law, for subduing the Law of the Mother. The Erinyes, the "mother's hounds," who uphold the old Law based on the belief that killing one's own mother is the most horrible crime, and that the murder of a husband is not "shedding of one's own blood" (Eumenides 212), are turned, through the agency of Orestes, into the complying Eumenides. They are given ground (a sacred grove) in the new order that declares the mother a stranger to her offspring (Eumenides 660). Patricide, on the other hand, confirms the Law of the Father through the retribution and final enlightenment of Oedipus. The dissymmetry of the two crimes acquires its mysterious balancing point when the transformation of Oedipus in Oedipus at Colonus takes place in the sacred grove of the Eumenides, that is, precisely on the ground that had been established through the justification of matricide.

And yet, the myth of Athena's motherlessness has deeper layers than what has been offered to us by Aeschylus in Oresteia. According to a rendering of the myth that precedes Aeschylus, Athena did have a mother, the goddess of wisdom Metis, who was swallowed by Zeus while she was pregnant. So far as Greek mythology is concerned, this was the decisive swallowing: Ouranos tried to keep his children in their mother's belly and was overthrown; Kronos wanted to keep them in his own belly and was overthrown. Only through the ingesting of the Mother did the Father finally achieve supremacy. In this way, Hesiod (1983) informs us, Zeus had Metis's council always at hand and could use it without having to recur to an Other (Theog. 900).

This, however, caused him a terrible headache: Athena was born out of a headache. Zeus instituted himself—the womb of patrilineariry, of the name of the Father, of the Father's huge bald forehead—leaving us the legacy of a cannibalistic culture forever trying to vomit the Mother whom it has swallowed in the first place. Having in mind that Athena did not initially belong to the Olympian pantheon, that she was, most probably, a goddess of Cretan and Mycenaean origin, and that her passage through Zeus's head was in this sense the act of her transfer from an earlier to a later epoch, and from one culture to another, we will be tempted to see Zeus's head as the occlusion of the hallucinatory osmosis of the daughter with the Minoan-Mycenaean mother.

It is out of this occlusion that the voice always mothered by absence enunciates its repetitive and solitary rebellion. But if the occlusion is dissolved and if, as Woolf's last sentence in A Room of One's Own runs, "Chloe likes Olivia . . . rather than fling an inkpot at her . . ." there might be a problem still. Of a different order. I turn to it in the next chapter.

5

Feminine Erotic and Paternal Legacy: Revisiting Plato's Symposium

FUSION AND REDUPLICATION

As already discussed, Julia Kristeva defines reduplication as the direct expression and the immediate language of female libido. Reduplication is a jammed repetition. It is a stammering of temporality that forever struggles to pronounce one and the same petrified moment. It is an eternal return of the same but unlike the return that is "rippled out in time," reduplication is a reverberation outside of time. It is, therefore, a spatial occurrence, yet even its spatiality is unstable and tends to collapse in "a play of mirrors lacking perspective or duration" (Kristeva 1989, p. 246).

In the previous chapter I focused on the abjective and matricidal manifestation of reduplication: the double emerges as the victorious murderer and the forgetful replica of an earlier, supposedly sinister writing that is incorpsed and thrown out of the body proper of literature. The result is a blocking of spatial and temporal discreteness that dooms the writing woman to be forever the first of her kind. Similar results may follow from a specific kind of amorous technique that can be described as fusional or symbiotic, or, indeed, osmotic *érotique du féminin*: mobilized in order to restore femininity to writing, it runs the risk of inadvertently eradicating alterity.

The impasse of reduplication is the necessity to tell murder from love. The fate of Diotima, the wise woman who speaks of the mysteries of love in the *Symposium*, will takes us, in what follows, to the mysteries of repeated attempts to have *her* murdered. Woolf, memorably, displaces her question in *A Room of One's Own*, the question as to why there is no tradition of the mothers, with that of why our mothers were so poor. Then she speaks about money and property. Yet is it really a displacement of the question or is it the same question, after all? The matter of "what matters who's speaking" is, according to Woolf, a matter of property. There is no solution to the dilemmas of feminine erotic—or writing—outside of the dilemmas of a legacy signed with the name of the father. Woolf's late and radical solutions to these dilemmas are explored in Chapter 6. Here I turn to the dilemmas around the name of Diotima.

EROTICS AND TEMPORALITY

In an ardent essay entitled "Irigaray at the *Symposium*: Speaking Otherwise" Barbara Freeman (1986) attempts to effect what other women (and Virginia Woolf among them) have tried to do before her: that is, engage Plato's dialogue in an exchange with a woman-reader and transpose his disquisitions on love into the dynamic of female desire. To achieve this, Freeman introduces an Irigarayan conceptualization of "thoroughly feminine desire"—a desire that infinitely desires its repetition, and is, simultaneously, always and immediately fulfilled through touching itself. The speechless flute girl whose exit marks the beginning of the discussion in the *Symposium* and Alcibiades's intoxication that brings the flute girls back and unsettles the discussion at the end of the dialogue are singled out as instances outlining this type of desire. Femininity becomes the site of a rhetorical excess that finds its dramaturgical focus in the festive figure of Alcibiades. Femininity is thus located with, arguably, the one irresistible man at the banquet, whose desirability emerges out of the coupling of the silent flute girl with Luce Irigaray's script. With this shift of emphasis that introduces "Irigaray at the *Symposium*" and sets off Alcibiades's rarely praised appeal, Freeman "rewrites" Plato's dialogue so as to make space for feminine sexual difference within philosophy.

Freeman's project thus seems to rely on two major circumstances. The first is the simultaneity of the gestures that open space for feminine difference and rewrite the master texts of the past. The second is the necessity for a feminine disquisition on love to begin with the problem of desire for texts. The inaugural question of such a hypothetical symposium would then be, "How does one desire (Plato's) text?" Through its unsettling and unappropriated margins runs Freeman's answer, through the excess of its festivity; so, although "he" does not give himself even when he does not give himself, there are still unintended gifts for the reading woman, and "there is indeed room in *this* Symposium for a thoroughly feminine desire" (Freeman 1986, p. 176).

Freeman's essay, however, is yet another instance of "I am the first of a new genus"—in this case, the first one to read Plato with a "thoroughly feminine desire." Even Irigaray who is the theoretical authority behind Freeman's approach is not perceived as a commentator of Plato (which she is). Irigaray is evoked as the immediate mirroring of Freeman's own desire: their voices merge, drawing the intoxicated Alcibiades and the silent flute girl into the same dissolving embrace. Is it because they "touch upon"? Because "the distinguishing feature of women's statements 'is one of continuity'"? Because of the specificity of feminine desire that is for "the proximate rather than for (the) property"? Because of a feminine erotic deployed through the text where "words join in the same way as do muscles and joints" (Freeman 1986, p. 174)?

Diotima, the only woman speaking (in a very mediated manner, to be sure) at the *Symposium* does not have much chance with Freeman. Freeman (1986) rejects her outright as "guardian of and spokesperson for Platonic truth" (p. 172). The relationship between Diotima and Platonic truth (whatever this truth might be conceived to be), however, is not so easy to determine. Rendered through several narrators before we have to consider Plato and the devious history of Platonic commentary, Diotima is not a figure to be easily "touched upon." Yet with her very dismissal, Freeman adds to the chronicle of Diotima's remoteness. For "Diotima is not the only example of a woman whose wisdom, especially about love, is reported in her absence by a man," wrote Luce Irigaray (1993, p. 20), the very woman in whose name Freeman rejects Diotima. How does feminine erotic deal with distance? Does the nature of a desire that is immediately fulfilled through touching itself preclude any reference to what is remote and elusive? Can it know time? One of the chief targets of Irigaray's critique of the existing order of things is the confinement of women to ahistoricity and to a continuous present (Whitford 1991). I will turn to what Irigaray herself has to say about Diotima, as well as to Kristeva and Woolf; and, in the unfolding the discussion, to Foucault and two of his followers whose reading of Plato throws additional light on Woolf's concern with the tradition of the mothers. But before I do so, I make a detour that examines some weird controversies to which Diotima's intricately mediated presence at the *Symposium* gave rise.

THE CASE OF DIOTIMA

Freeman's proposal to uncover the site of difference in the *Symposium* is inscribed within a tradition of diverse attempts to do so—or, alternatively, to foreclose the possibility for doing so. Concerned as it is with a "pederastic" Eros, this dialogue is nevertheless perceived as possessing or being haunted by a feminine side that has to be conjured or exorcized. But where exactly is this feminine side to be located? Is it with Phaedrus's myth of a fatherless god of love, whose genesis is situated in an uncertain proximity to the "broad-bosomed Earth"? Is it with Pausanias's myth, which, reversing Phaedrus's story, speaks of a motherless goddess of love, who issued from a heavenly father? Is it with Aristophanes's myth of androgyny, which posits an original union? Is it with Diotima's myth of Poros and Penia, which posits an utter disparity, a drastic contrast? Is it with Agathon's "softness"? Is it with Alcibiades's rhetoric? Or is it with the ambiguities of Socrates himself, the "phallic mother," as Sarah Kofman (1989, p. 46) describes him, presiding at the all-male disquisition on love—appropriating as he does the language of female generative power in his intellectual maieusis and offering his own speech as a dialogic exchange with a woman?

And what about this woman, Diotima? The very mention of her name brings up insoluble questions. There is, to be sure, the case of Socrates, but there is also the less voluminous but no less intricate case of Diotima. The case of Socrates grows out of the question, What is the true Socratic teaching? It thus grounds Occidental philosophizing in the reading of the Unwritten, in the absence of the Father's writing that has incessantly to be filled in for him. Although there are exceptions, two of which will be discussed further on (they concern Roger Godel and Barbara Ehlers), the case of Diotima presents an altogether different question: Did Diotima exist? Is there a woman in Plato's text?

The case of Socrates focuses on the absence of a provable text, while the case of Diotima focuses on the absence of a provable body. Evoked at a banquet where everybody else has always been more or less unproblematically assumed as real and historical, Diotima tends to produce anxiety with her uncertain status. Was there such a woman? Did she exist? Taylor believes her to have existed but although there is nothing overstated about his view,[1] it is not often shared. We know nothing about her outside of Plato's dialogue, which tells us that she was a Mantinean priestess and that by offering sacrifice to the gods she delayed the plague in Athens for ten years. Whether she existed or not, is she a "guardian of and spokesperson for Platonic truth"? Discriminating between a true Socratic and an untrue sophistic Diotimean teaching, Wilamowitz-Moellendorff (1920) believes she is not. But even if she is not, why—to echo David Halperin's (1990) formulation of the question in the title of his essay—is Diotima a woman?

If she is, that is. The impulse to uncover Dion of Syracuse under Diotima's name (Neumann 1965), far from being an oddity, is only the most literal of the attempts to "unwoman" the Mantinean priestess. Rather than conjure Dion of Syracuse, however, most commentators maintain in some form that Diotima is a thinly disguised Plato. Diotima does stand for Platonic truth, runs this view, and precisely for that reason it does not matter whether there ever was a woman by that name, or not. Why a woman then? For rhetorical or psychological reasons; for example, Socrates's irony: "The question-and-answer method is *her* specialty!" (Guthrie 1986, p. 385).[2] Or, Socrates's concern for Agathon's pride glossed by Cornford (1950) as a "masterstroke of delicate courtesy" (p. 71). Or, Socrates's fidelity to the dialogic form. And yet, why should Plato hand over his truth to a woman? In fact, he did not. The necessity is to have Diotima as this or that man and yet, to not have her stand for Platonic truth. Rosen puts this most succinctly, "Diotima is not a thinly disguised Plato, but a purified Agathon, generated by the bisexual dialectic of Socrates" (Rosen 1968, p. 203). The latest versions have moved from considerations of psychology or rhetoric to con-

---

1. "I cannot agree with many modern scholars in regarding Diotima of Mantinea as a fictitious personage; still less in looking for fanciful reasons for giving the particular names Plato does to the prophetess and her place of origin. The introduction of purely fictitious named personages into a discourse seems to be a literary device unknown to Plato . . . and I do not believe that if he had invented Diotima he would have gone on to put into the mouth of Socrates the definite statement that she had delayed the pestilence of the early years of the Archidamian war for ten years by 'offering sacrifice' at Athens" (Taylor 1963, p. 224).

2. Ergo, Socrates is being ironic and Diotima did not exist.

siderations of the politics of gender. The results, however, are similar: they try to conjure away Diotima. Freeman (1986) joins these attempts by pointing out that "woman can be a symbol of truth or wisdom, like Diotima, as long as those doing the actual desiring or truth-seeking are men" (p. 171) and Halperin, to whom I will return, offers a sophisticated detour toward a tropological and quintessentially masculine Diotima whose difference serves to legitimize the regime of the same. At an extreme end, outlining the logical limits of the enigma, all questions pertaining to Diotima's presence in Plato's dialogue receive a negative answer. It does not matter whether Diotima existed, and if it does, well, she did not exist, and if she did, well, she does not stand for Plato's truth, and if she does, well, she is not a woman, and if she is, Plato's truth is passé anyway.

The curious question of why the very presence of Diotima has caused so much controversy is very much the question that drives the quest in this book. The problem that the fictional and tropological views on Diotima face and solve with singular nonchalance is setting Diotima apart from the reality of the other participants in the dialogue and from the reality of Socrates who, after all, is "generated by the bisexual dialectic of Plato" as the founding fiction of Occidental philosophizing. There is an obvious difficulty here and many of the commentators take special care to ensure that Diotima is a literary device of the second order; that she, so to say, is the trope of a trope, the "fictional double" (Guthrie 1986, p. 385) of a fiction, and, as the poet has put it, the dream of a shadow. Socrates's story is reversed. Instead of a young man instructed by a priestess within concrete spatial and temporal settings, we end up with an old man inventing a literary heroine—and a male one at that. A double movement is hence effected through which Diotima is still further derealized, while Socrates, although carefully framed by Plato's narrators, turns into a criterion of historical reality. "Depleted by Socrates, she vanishes, but Socrates's erotic wisdom and his entrancing speeches endure" (Halperin 1990, p. 148). She vanishes because of Socrates's entrancing speeches? Because of Plato's writings? Or because of Platonic commentary? In what way do we determine the precise point where reality turns into fiction, enduring turns into depletion, and writing dissolves into the irretrievable horizon of speaking? There must be something remarkably tenacious about Diotima's vanishing if the effort to prove her a nonentity still has to be renewed. What necessitates this effort? Why do commentators need Diotima not to be (a woman)?

RUIN AS FORM

The stubborn quality about Diotima's never quite final depletion emerges also out of the rare attempts to sidestep the uncertainties of the Platonic text and confirm the woman in it through evidence taken from without. In a study that Friedländer (1958) describes as "worth-while reading though fanciful," (p. 365, n. 14), Roger Godel (1955) grapples with Socrates's initiation in the secrets of love by Diotima, and with the problem of what conjectures we might make on the subject. In a fittingly tentative and fragmentary fashion he proceeds to give some information on the Mantinean wise women, philosophers and mystics, on the Mantinean cults of the subterranean Demeter, the black Aphrodite and the infernal Dionysus, and on the suggestive Arcadian landscape. We are thus first induced to place Diotima amidst this profound scenery, in the evocative precincts of temples and sanctuaries. After that we are invited to follow Diotima on her way to Athens and to try to guess in what temple she may have stayed there, in what surroundings her conversations with Socrates may have taken place. It is suggested that Socrates may have met her in the settings of Plato's other great dialogue on love, *Phaedrus*. She is introduced in that other dialogue, therefore, in the form of a landscape and this is very much what has remained of her as a result of Godel's imaginative reconstruction: a collection of probable landscapes, a chart of a mystical journey.

In an altogether different approach to the case of Diotima, Barbara Ehlers (1966) offers a reading of the remaining fragments of Aischines's dialogue *Aspasia*. She places the fragments in the context of other philosophical or nonphilosophical works and, through the reconstruction of Aischines's meaning, tries to give an answer to the questions of (1) the content of a pre-Platonic rendering of the Socratic Eros; (2) its possible origin with Aspasia, the wise hetaera whose dubious image has reached us via the scanty and contentious testimony of the philosophers and the comedians; and (3) the similarity of this pre-Platonic Eros with the Eros in the teaching of Diotima who thus becomes Aspasia disguised by Plato in order to avoid the unpleasant associations with the comedians' portrayal of the hetaera. In this way Ehlers undertakes the difficult task not only of establishing an unshakable historical alibi for the existence of Diotima, but also of outlining her teaching. The meticulous and exhaustive reclaiming of Aspasia that the study effects is outstanding. The result, however, is that instead of one woman of whom we know little, we get another one about whom our knowledge is very problematic. The question is why we should exchange the one for the other at all. Reversing the order of Ehlers's remarkable effort, we may see Plato's Diotima fragmented into the controversial comic and philosophic variants of Aspasia and then into the aporias of a text only partially preserved. Both Godel's "fanciful" recreation of Diotima in terms of a collection of landscapes and Ehlers's struggle against the odds of lost texts and contradictory reports result in a heap of bits and pieces.

This is also what happens if we take the Eleusinian mysteries as a point of departure. Although the discernible allusions to the language of the mysteries in Diotima's speech are few and uncertain due to the secrecy that was part of the Eleusinian experience, it is sometimes believed that the very structure of the dialogue as well as its "dramatic date" point toward Eleusis (Morgan 1990). Inconclusive as the evidence for such a reading is, if we approach it for an answer to the case of Diotima, the result will be once again to explain an enigma with another one, more baffling than the first. Although bits and pieces continue to be put together, "the secret of the Mysteries *was kept a secret* successfully and we shall perhaps never be able to fathom it or unravel it" (Mylonas 1961, p. 281). To explain Diotima with Eleusis is to transfer the riddle from the priestess to the goddess.

The perplexities that accompany the case of Diotima have been reproduced in the visual arts. There is an attic relief that has been interpreted by Hans Moebius as Diotima since it represents a priestess, a diviner with liver in her hand; it was probably the work of an Athenian sculptor from around the time of Socrates's story and it was found in Mantinea. Even if we accept this evidence, the image is broken. Another relief representing an ugly satyr-like man conversing with a woman, with the figure of Eros between them, is sometimes interpreted as a conversation between Socrates and Diotima (Schefold 1943). It is not at all certain, however, that the man is Socrates, and the woman, judging by the details, seems to be a hetaera rather than a priestess. Diotima alias Aspasia again?

A landscape rich in archaeological bits and pieces, a broken image, a damaged text, a cult with a lost secret: outside of Plato's dialogue Diotima remains at least as problematic as inside it. There is a mother, a feminine presence, a wise woman professionally knowledgeable (whether as a priestess, as a hetaera, or, indeed, as the goddess herself) in the mysteries of Eros. Her traces can be detected both inside and outside of Plato's *Symposium*. Yet it cannot be argued with any degree of certainty where or who precisely she is. The attempt to look closer at her results in the shifting and shattering of her coordinates, or into her transformation into somebody else. Fragmentation and disguise characterize this presence with an uncertain locus. If we try to situate the case of Diotima (or is it Aspasia?) between the fragments of Sappho, as the one message from a speaking woman that precedes her, and Hypatia, of whom nothing has remained but the story of her great learning and of her murder at the end of Antiquity by an overzealous Christian crowd that virtually tore her to pieces, we might find some systematic or even necessary character in the uncertainty and the fragmentation. The woman at the site where Western culture has repeatedly returned in search of its constructions or deconstructions will remain, however, unlocatable. A *mater abscondita*.

JULIA KRISTEVA: FROM EROS TO TOKOS

And yet, there is the phenomenon that Benjamin (1977) described as the vitality and the indestructible meaningfulness of the fragment. Diotima's case posits the necessity to live through the past ruin as the form of our present, and through fracture as the totality of meaning. It uncovers the horizon of our inescapably baroque vision that can experience wholeness only as a retrospective mirage. From this point of view Diotima is the truth of Socrates and Socrates with his enduring speeches is a Diotima thickly disguised by centuries of pious reconstruction. Confronting Diotima's fragmented tenacity in the face of depletion, therefore, we confront the very paradox of our historicity.

There is, in Plato's dialogue, a linguistic double to this tenacity of the fragment. In Diotima's speech, as has often been observed, there is a cluster of words that relates the productivity of Eros, its creative drive and its ultimate justification, to pregnancy, genesis, parturition, giving birth, and nourishing. This language evoking female generative power and centering around the conceptualization of birth, *tokos*,[3] is manifest at all stages of Diotima's discourse. In the myth about Poros and Penia with which Diotima undertakes initially to explain the nature of Eros to Socrates, the emphasis is not simply on the mode of Eros's birth, resulting as it does from the copulation of wealth and poverty, lack and abundance, drowsiness and vigil, and so on. The emphasis is also on the cunning desire for giving birth. The

---

3. For a discussion of the various translations of *tokos*, see Schmid (1987).

birth of Eros is thus preceded by the craving or indeed the plotting and the scheming for giving birth by Penia.[4] This change of emphasis is reasserted in Diotima's discussion of the lesser mysteries of love. What could explain the *mania* of love, the ravenous pursuit of the beloved, the madness of desire? According to Diotima the longing to give "birth in beauty" is the hidden drive behind erotic frenzy. Both the enigma of the lover's desire and the secret of the beloved's attraction can be explained through delivery and procreation. From this point on, Diotima's speech systematically intertwines Eros and *tokos*. Souls get pregnant the way bodies do. Beauty is the goddess of parturition. Each moment we give birth to ourselves in bodily and spiritual terms. Birth as the generation of copies explains the operation of memory and the resulting preservation of identity in a world of mutability. All human activity—from the poet's inspiration to the politician's concerns—is fecundity, giving birth. Giving birth is our mortal analogue to immortality, what brings us closest to the gods. In a final reiteration of the *tokos* theme Diotima formulates the highest stage of the greater mysteries of love as the giving birth and nourishing of virtue that makes the human being "the friend of God." From its manifestation as desire and lack to its ultimate realization as the search for truth and the contemplation of divine beauty, Eros in Diotima's account is superseded by *tokos*.

Diotima's introduction of the theme of *tokos* marks her departure from the speakers before her. So does her understanding of Eros as a great demon of mediation, as the intermediary between poverty and wealth, knowledge and ignorance, ugliness and beauty, mortality and immortality. Eros is not beautiful, wise, or immortal, as the rest of the speakers would have him, but something in-between. In this in-betweenness where each of the lovers looks for what he lacks there emerges the togetherness undermining the dichotomy of lover and beloved, of active subject and passive object of desire, which figures prominently in some of the preceding speeches and which receives its paradoxical twist in Alcibiades's encomium. This togetherness replacing the lover/beloved dissymmetry turns the amorous couple toward the pursuit of the good and the true and generates its common offspring, be it material or spiritual, as the work, the *ergon* of love.

Thus, love in Plato's dialogue carries out the transition from the discourse of desire to the discourse of knowledge in its capacity as a demon-

---

4. For a fascinating discussion of Penia's aporia as the beginning of philosophical inquiry, see Kofman (1983).

mediator and Eros-as-tokos. Traditionally, this transition, this "birth in beauty," has been interpreted as the transcendence of carnal heterosexual love by the ideal Platonic love, and as the superseding of the female creativity of the flesh by the male creativity of the spirit. Marsilio Ficino's commentary on Plato's *Symposium*, which played a crucial role in inscribing Plato's ideas in the European Rennaissance, offers precisely this filtering of Plato's text. With Ficino, in fact, the dichotomy becomes so insurmountable that the base love of the flesh is taken out completely from the concept of love: enjoyment and pleasure, according to Ficino, pertain to the mind, vision, and hearing; the attraction affecting the other senses is seen as lust and excess. It is an abuse of love to transfer to embraces and touching feelings that should be concerned only with sight and contemplation. According to this voyeuristic reading of Plato the love of the flesh is valueless; it is only the fecundity of the spirit that deserves the name of love.

This hierarchical ordering of the fertility of the body and the amorous ideality—no matter whether it is perceived as a triumph of male spirituality, or as a legitimation of homosexual practices—is questioned in Kristeva's reading of the *Symposium*. Diotima's emphasis on mediation, togetherness, and fecundity is not the result of the evolution, or transcendence, or replacement of carnal (female) fecundity by sublime spiritual (male) love. What happens, conceptually speaking, when Diotima takes the floor in the *Symposium* is rather the introduction, within the manic and extreme dynamic of the male libido, of a different amorous universe, a simultaneous lateral space of an alien libidinal economy. Diotima provides a maternal emphasis on unity rather than possession, on mediation and synthesis rather than the master–slave strife, and on procreation rather than pleasure; with such an emphasis, Diotima enters, according to Kristeva (1987b, p. 59), the "sado-masochistic psychodrama under the shadow of the phallus" with a message that desexualizes Eros, that curbs its death-driven, agonistic economy, and relocates it on the way to "phallic idealization." Her discourse is hence concerned with the transmutation of the violent and manic male libido. It marks the point of the transformation of Eros—turning him into the very mediating demon of this transformation—into Pteros. The "devastating possession" turns into "an idealizing bird caught in the rising motion of the soul." This transition effected by Eros-as-tokos "shackles the death drive and acts as a counterbalance to death." It "allows less to repress than to separate raving desire from its refinement, from its dialectic and academic education on behalf of the city-state" (p. 76).

In the later dialogue, *Phaedrus*, this transition, this point of transmutation has become invisible—sunk into the landscape, as Godel believes? For the time being, however, in the *Symposium*, the sublime vision is rendered as an "intellectual transposition of a pagan jouissance, the dazzlement of maternal fertility" (Kristeva 1987b, p. 74). "Phallic idealization" is thus the offshoot of the master–slave dialectic, of the power relationships and the sadomasochistic violence of the pederastic Eros *and* a mediatory, reconciliatory, and maieutic gesture that comes from elsewhere. What is transcended is not the carnality of female creativity but the erotic mania obsessed with power, dominion, and death. The feminine, maternal emphasis on creativity and unity exhibits the heterogeneity that mediates and sustains this transcendence. In his study of the ways in which ritual and religious belief have been transposed by Plato for the needs of philosophy, Michael Morgan (1990) seems to express a similar idea by stating that, in the *Symposium*, "the mysteries of Eleusis mediate between Bacchic frenzy and philosophy" (p. 99). In a similar vein, according to Kristeva (1987b), "it is as if a goddess, a woman were needed to desexualize love" (p. 72): the first Platonist, the first proponent of a sublime love motivated by an ideal supracelestial pursuit is, within this setting, necessarily a woman. Addressing Plato's text as a process of generation traversing the spaces between the manic and the sublime, Kristeva reaches a conclusion that might support, from an entirely different perspective, Ehlers's philological inquiry: there is a woman behind Socrates's doctrine of Eros.

WHY IS DIOTIMA A MAN

The point is not simply to restate once again that phallic power begins with an appropriation of archaic maternal power. The point is also to confront the question about the stakes in ignoring or glossing over this appropriation as always already consumed and hence *bound only to be reproduced.* What is the exigency behind the recurring attempts to disregard or omit Diotima, ranging, as we have seen, from the insistence on her fictionality (as something set against the reality of the other speakers in the *Symposium*) to the inevitable effort to see her as a man?

Diotima is never problematized in Foucault's (1985) *History of Sexuality.* His narrative of the purely economic status of Greek women and of the emergence of the discourse on truth and knowledge out of a thoroughly male pedagogy never addresses the implications of Diotima's presence. Foucault does not explain why there should be a woman in the male pedagogic setting where, according to his presentation, the concern with the boy's honor and with the tensions and inequalities of the pederastic Eros becomes the single driving force for the transition from the problematic of *aphrodisia*, the "use of the pleasures," to the problematic of truth. Foucault, in other words, avoids the question that, as was already pointed out, vexed numerous Platonic scholars and that was formulated by David Halperin as "Why is Diotima a woman?" This silence is especially prominent because of the emphasis he lays on the maleness of the transition.

The stubbornness of the case of Diotima, however, is manifested once again. The moment it is totally ignored it reenters the discussion because of this very omission—not necessarily in the spirit of disapproval but also in the spirit of sympathy and consent. This is what happens in Wilhelm Schmid's *The Birth of Philosophy in the Garden of Desire: Michael Foucault's Archeology of the Platonic Eros* (1987) and in David Halperin's "Why Is Diotima a Woman?" (1990). Fully aware of the enormity of Foucault's omission of Diotima, Schmid and Halperin undertake its theoretical justification. Their justifications, however, lead to difficulties that emphasize once more the inevitability of Diotima.

As already mentioned, the transition, summarized in the phrase "birth in beauty," has been traditionally interpreted as the transcendence of carnal heterosexual love by the ideal Platonic homosexual love, and as the superseding of the female creativity of the flesh by the male creativity of the spirit. In his study of Foucault, Schmid makes the plausible assumption that this traditional interpretation is what Foucault wants to avoid through the omission of Diotima. However, Schmid also believes Diotima to be indispensible for the Platonic project. Consequently, Schmid offers a discussion of *tokos*, as employed in Plato's *Symposium*, and of its translations in different languages, and he reads Foucault's inattention to this unavoidable aspect of Plato's dialogue as being dictated by a deplatonizing project. Foucault, Schmid tells us, has no use for the Platonic absolutes that emerge out of Diotima's discourse and that are mediated by her language of procreation. His concern is with the use of the pleasures and not with their sublime transfromations. Hence the removal of Diotima—the de-diotimization of the *Symposium*—is equivalent to de-platonization: it is a critique of the idealizing and logocentric aspects of Platonic thought.

In this respect Schmid shares Barbara Freeman's views: for him, Diotima is guardian of and spokesperson for Platonic truth. It is noteworthy that the proponents of Platonic truth (whatever this truth might be found to be) tend to dissociate Diotima from this truth, while the opponents of Platonic truth tend to associate it with her. Schmid's account, however, fails to recognize the fact that Foucault's revision of habitual interpretations of Plato is concerned not with the end where the idealizing Platonic concepts appear, but rather with the beginnings of these concepts, with the site of their production. Foucault is not interested in critiquing Platonic idealizations, although what he wants to do with them is, indeed, a very curious question in the light of his late writing. It is unquestionable, however, that he tries to retrace the processes that lead to these idealizations. Hence he is interested not in removing them but in following the ascetic measures that lead to them—that is, the preservation of these idealizations is, for Foucault, a heuristic necessity. The concepts of true love, and of the love of the true, do not transpose the city's concern with procreation. Rather, and this is Foucault's point, they are transpositions of the city's concern with the honor of boys, of the future free citizens. How is today's passive boy to be legitimized as tomorrow's active citizen? This was the question confronting Athena; not the question of how to legitimize the nonproductive homosexual relationships. It is not carnal heterosexual love that is transcended, as the view quoted by Schmid would have it; it is the problematic of the love for boys that is transformed. Foucault's emphasis, therefore, is on the emergence of the discourse of truth out of the tensions of homosexual relationships; on the workings of a *subjectivation* based on an aesthetics of *aphrodisia* rather than on a hermeneutics of desire; and on the ethical work contingent on the stylization of freedom rather than on the interiorization of interdictions.

Foucault approaches the *Symposium* as indicative of this *ethical work*, this scene of production that preoccupies him. By contending that these processes and transitions might not be that easily disengaged from Diotima's presence, and that Diotima is implicated in the movement toward what Foucault himself defines as a joint access to truth, Schmid restores the *tokos* dimension of the emerging discourses that interest Foucault and in practice jeopardizes Foucault's project to describe this emergence as male only.

Halperin seems to share Schmid's view of the significance of Diotima's omission by Foucault, but is also careful not to compromise Foucault's perspective. He takes an altogether different route. If Foucault says nothing about a woman in Plato's dialogue, it is because there is no woman in this dialogue. Diotima is a man. Ostensibly, she explains the mystery of Eros, which the previous speakers in the *Symposium* tackle, through the desire to give birth. In fact, her very notion of giving birth is modeled on erotic pleasure. Reversing Diotima's rhetorical movement from Eros to *tokos*, Halperin translates back her discourse of procreation into the discourse of erotics. Now pregnancies turn into erections, parturitions turn into ejaculations, and the phantasmatic babies that spring forth with so much zest return Diotima's emphasis on creativity into the economy of pleasure. The birth in beauty is a coming into beauty, after all.

The ravishing apparition of such exuberant labors re-masculinizes Diotima. Halperin displaces, but also retains, Diotima's ambiguities in a seductive figure that, according to him, demonstrates a double movement effected by Greek culture. This double movement at first estranges procreation from the concept of male sexuality in the Greek construction of gender and then, via Plato's ventriloquism of Diotima's voice, reappropriates it. There is a definitive male sexuality that can be found on any side in the construction of gender divisions: whether she gives birth in beauty or, indeed, ejaculates in it, Diotima is a man.

Halperin (1990), therefore, does not stop with seduction; he has to prove that Diotima is the man he has turned her into. Thus, although there is no genuinely feminine experience that can be specified, there is a "form of sexual experience which is masculine to begin with" (p. 142). The masculine sexual experience finds its expression precisely in Diotima's seemingly female language of procreation, for the "interdependence of sexual and reproductive capacities is in fact a feature of male, not female physiology" (p. 142). Hence "Plato's figuration of Diotima's supposed 'femininity' reinscribes male identity in the representation of female 'difference'" (p. 145).

A pause seems to be necessary at this point. Is there, indeed, an "interdependence of sexual and reproductive capacities" in male physiology, and whatever might such an interdependence mean? If erotic pleasure (but then to what extent?) is a condition for a man to be able to procreate, is procreation a condition for him to be able to have pleasure? If everything that a man can do about reproduction is come, is it also true that everything he can do about coming is reproduce? It seems that, contrary to Halperin's delightful phantasm, there is no definitive interdependence, no biconditional equivalence of the connection between sexual and reproductive capacities in either male sexuality or Diotima's teaching. If men have to desire in order to be able to procreate, they certainly do not *have* to procreate in order to be able to desire. Yet Diotima implies precisely this second dependence: it is the drive for procreation that propels erotic frenzy. We may do whatever we like with this mystery (as we shall presently see, Irigaray offers a mutuality of eroticism and fecundity of a very different type); we may keep silent about it, as Foucault did, but we cannot equate it with the paradigmatic physiological truth of male sexuality. For the first result of such an equation would be to render nonprocreational male homosexuality unthinkable, as Plato remembered very well, and as Halperin obviously forgot in the process of unwomaning Diotima.

Both Schmid's and Halperin's attempts to explicate Foucault's silence about Diotima end up obscuring Foucault's perspective. Schmid does this by undercutting Foucault's interest in the "stylization of freedom" that transforms the erotic pursuit into a pursuit of truth; Halperin, by dissolving Plato's logic into a phantasmatic physiology, thus inadvertently invalidating the homosexual relation, which for both Plato and Foucault, is the scene where the birth, *tokos*, of the search for knowledge is effected. There remains the problem about the never-ending attempts to remove Diotima from this site of the birth of philosophy. If she has always already been depleted by Socratic erotic wisdom, as Halperin contends, reminding us of the swallowing of Metis by Zeus, why has the depletion to be constantly resumed? Are we facing, perhaps, a phallogocentrism that, far from being handed down to us pure and simple from the beginning— or, for that matter, from Plato on—is, in fact, constantly and vigilantly retrojected? Retrojected from the (always-at-last-attentive-to-the-question-of-woman) present to a past that, nevertheless, cannot be reduced to such totalizations?

VIRGINIA WOOLF: LIKE WATERS POURED INTO ONE JAR

On the other hand, we might ask ourselves whether Kristeva's vision of the sublime pederastic Eros is not in fact a woman's phantasm about male sexuality—extreme, bestial, and tragic even (or most of all) in its ideal supracelestial pursuits? Could we, perhaps, see this vision as an estrangement of female sexuality, which is first delegated "in the shadow of the phallus" and then reappropriated through the foregrounding of Diotima? Could this foregrounding be Kristeva's specific angle for uncovering the seductiveness of Plato's text?

In her conceptualization of Plato's sadomasochistic Eros as corresponding to the dynamic of the male libido, Kristeva proceeds from Freud's belief in the existence of one libido only, male. She then intercedes with the question, Could we nevertheless speak of a female libido, of a purely feminine erotic? If the answer is yes, then this erotic might be described as "that opening-closing, blossoming-wilting, an in-between hardly established that suddenly collapses into the same warmth" (Kristeva 1987b, p. 81). Although designated as male and female, both libidinal economies are underwritten by a scientific myth that drafts a space outside of gender division. So, as Kristeva reiterates, Freud anchors the morbid, manic and destructive aspects of Eros "in the prehistory of matter that propagated by means of scission before having acquired an organ with erotic and procreative functions" (p. 79); while Kristeva, on her part, relates the lethal, depersonalizing tendency of the feminine erotic to the "loving dialogue of the pregnant mother with the fruit, barely distinct from her, that she shelters in her womb" (p. 81). There is a paradox involved in both cases: the scission is death that may turn out to be the way for the cell's procreation; the womb is life that may turn into a "grinding death" for those who refuse separation.

Both libidinal economies are, therefore, anchored in a crux of destructiveness and generation that is as yet ignorant of the dramas of sex and gender. To these models, as Kristeva makes clear, any type of individual relationship, homosexual or heterosexual, might have any type of correlation. The two models, however, are not symmetrical. They refer to different moments in the formation of the subject and tell disparate stories about the "lost territory" (of the mother) that constitutes us as speaking beings, and about the processes that check the death drive and open the roads for idealization. If the pederastic Eros is destructive, it is also a powerful "bird of idealization"; if, deployed as a sexuality in itself, female libido is precarious, it also grounds the potentialities of love. And the two economies modify each other through interaction. As a mediator in the dramaturgy of male libido, feminine love provides the turning point in Plato's *Symposium*; and later on, according to Kristeva's reading of Plotinus in *Tales of Love*, it becomes the agent of an incarnation of Platonic absolute beauty that brings about the emergence of psychic space and forms the basis of Occidental internality and self-reflexivity. The differences and dissymmetries do not mean, therefore, that the two models differ in terms of their ultimate value or ethos: Kristeva insists on the troubled and hazardous labor of Eros, on the *ergon* of love.

And this is precisely the viewpoint from which Virginia Woolf reads the *Symposium* in *To the Lighthouse*. In a study of the Platonic references in this novel, Jean Wyatt (1978) identifies a passage in terms of its allusions to the late coming of Socrates in the *Symposium*, when Agathon invites him to take the place next to him so that

"I may touch you," he said, "and have the benefit of that wise thought which came into your mind in the portico, and is now in your possession. . . ." "How I wish," said Socrates, taking his place as he was desired, "that wisdom could be infused by touch, out of the fuller into the emptier man, as water runs through wool out of a fuller cup into an emptier one; if that were so, how greatly should I value the privilege of reclining at your side!" [Plato 1953, pp. 175d–e]

This playful exchange about the desire and the impossibility of an immediate transmission of knowledge is, of course, an introduction to the discussion that Socrates will crown with Diotima's message, according to which Eros is the *daemon* of mediation and ideality, and which Alcibiades will expand with the story of another Socratic lesson on the chances of infusing wisdom by touch. Woolf's reference to this passage is clearly recognizable and yet strangely distorted. Lily Briscoe, the artist struggling for her work, is pressing against Mrs. Ramsay's knees, imagining how in this beautiful woman whom she is physically touching, there stand, "like the treasures in the tombs of kings, tablets bearing sacred inscriptions" (Woolf 1927, p. 59). She then goes on to ask,

What art was there, known to love or cunning, by which one pressed through into those secret chambers? What device for becoming, like waters poured into one jar, inextricably the same, one with the object one adored? Could the body achieve it, or the mind, subtly mingling in the intricate passages of the brain? or the heart? Could loving, as people called it, make her and Mrs. Ramsay one? for it was not knowledge but unity that she desired, not inscriptions on tablets, nothing that could be written in any language known to men, but intimacy itself, which is knowledge. . . . Nothing happened. Nothing! Nothing! [p. 60]

The passage, while clearly hinting at the Socrates–Agathon joke about the transfusion of wisdom, is remarkable for its compression of several motives from the *Symposium*. Like Penia, Lily Briscoe craves through love or cunning to avail herself of the Poros-like fullness of Mrs. Ramsay. Like Agathon, she dreams of knowledge through bodily touch. Like Aristophanes's halflings, she desires to become one with her. Like Pausanias's follower of the heavenly Aphrodite, she is ready to give up the body for the unity with the mind. And, finally, like Alcibiades, she concludes in exasperation: "Nothing happened. Nothing! Nothing!"

There is an awesome quality about this very denseness of the quotation. It is as if the interplay of different voices that the *Symposium* offers, the togetherness of distinct views on love, have been fused again in this moment of mute intoxicated touch, and reversed in a single movement toward the pulsation of the drive. For days after this experience, we are told, about Lily Briscoe there hangs "the sound of murmuring," and she is haunted by the vision of the "murmurs and stirrings" of innumerable lives glued together by a "sweetness or sharpness" in a "dome-shaped hive" (Woolf 1927, p. 60). Strange collapses and uncertainties spell out Lily's desire while she presses against Mrs. Ramsay's knee: Does she want union because she wants knowledge, or does she crave the sacred inscriptions because she craves intimacy? She finally refuses to differentiate between the two. Her hesitation between the body and the mind as the means to achieve her yearning tips over into the clinical image of a mind "subtly mingling in the intricate passages of the brain." In a striking remodeling, Socrates's metaphor of the full and the empty cup is rendered by Lily's "waters poured into one jar." The two containers have been replaced by one; the dissymmetries and inequalities, the tensions and anxieties about having and not having, the oppositions (of full and empty, of liquid and dry) that characterize the master–slave dialectic of the male libido, and that surface in the jokingly agonistic exchange between Socrates and Agathon, as well as in Socrates's metaphor itself, have disappeared into the image of unnumbered plenitudes; they have united, like waters, without remnant, and have become "inextricably the same." Meanwhile no words are exchanged between Mrs. Ramsay and Lily. They do not speak; they touch. Body and mind intermingled, language and intimacy merged, boundaries blurred, liquid identities become indistinguishable, murmurs and stirrings dissolved in the "sharpness or sweetness" of the air; we are in the domain of the "mechanic of fluids," in the perilous and jubilatory realm of the feminine erotic.

An embodiment of beauty and love, of the opulence of being, of earthly fecundity and the promise of supra-celestial revelations, with a philosopher as her husband and the lighthouse as her symbol, Mrs. Ramsay is in herself a citation from the pages of Western philosophy. She is Diotima as the "symbol of wisdom or truth," a phallic mother, an inspirer of thought and a giver of visions. By quoting this figure from the *Symposium* into her own text and making the woman-artist in search of her work face it, Virginia Woolf re-eroticizes Plato's dialogue from a male into a female libidinal setting, very much in the way that Freeman proposes. Plato's text is disclosed as perilously seductive, as laden with the dangers of an amorous intoxication that dissolves its sacred inscriptions into an intimacy that is equated with knowledge. For the woman-reader, it turns out, the presence of Diotima has an impact quite the reverse of its impact on the male symposium: instead of effecting, with its mediating gesture, the transition to ideality, this presence reveals the text as charged with the longing to return to the body and to the pulsations of a primordial unity. With Alcibiades's exasperated "nothing happened," Woolf makes Lily Briscoe go back to the lessons of Socratic pedagogy.

From that point on, the movement of the novel may be regarded as the elaboration and accumulation of impediments and mediations, of distancing devices to be set between Lily Briscoe and the impossible proximity of her desire. The title should not blind us to the fact that Lily goes to the lighthouse by proxy—by not going there. For her achieved *ergon* at the end, so much depends, as she herself puts it at some point, upon distance. The novel is about distancing, not about oneness and approximation. Time passes. Mrs. Ramsay dies. The war changes the world. And there is Mr. Ramsay, the philosopher whose concern is with "a kitchen table . . . when you are not there" (Woolf 1927, p. 28). When, toward the end, the ghostly Mrs. Ramsay appears, as good as the living one, knitting the unending stockings—a horror with which Woolf was all too familiar—it is quite understandable why Lily should feel the need for the specialist on "subject and object and the nature of reality." "Where was the boat now? Mr. Ramsay? She wanted him" (p. 230).

And yet, Mr. Ramsay, the man who never gives but always takes, is a puny substitute, in the drama of the female libido, for the bounteous figure of Diotima. We know what Woolf thought of her father on whom Mr. Ramsay was modeled—that had he lived, there would have been "no books" (Woolf 1953, p. 137). Beyond Mr. Ramsay, however, there is, as we have seen, the allure of the *Symposium* itself and, with it, the allure of the "well-sunned nature, [of] the man who practices the art of living to the best advantage," and who makes us "seek truth with every part of us" (Woolf 1925b, p. 52). Like the flute-girl, sent away in order to return as Diotima, Mr. Ramsay's modest presence seems to usher in the grandeur of Plato. A similar process is going on in *A Room of One's Own* where contemporary novelists are deplored for being too masculine, but the inspirational androgynous splendor of Shakespeare is evoked. Later on, with *Three Guineas* and *Between the Acts*, Woolf seems to have despaired of this imaginary mediation.

LUCE IRIGARAY: THE DAIMON-MEDIATOR

Irigaray's essay "Sorcerer Love: A Reading of Plato, *Symposium*, Diotima's Speech" appeared in French in 1984, one year before Barbara Freeman presented her own essay at a philosophical symposium. Freeman does not refer to Irigaray's essay—she refers to the English translation of *This Sex Which Is Not One*, which had just been published at the time. The difference between Irigaray's reading of the *Symposium* according to Freeman and Irigaray's own reading of the *Symposium* is fascinating. Far from rejecting Diotima as the symbol of wisdom and the guardian of and spokesperson for Platonic truth, Irigaray—much more radically than I dare do here—postulates, beyond Socrates's male report, the erotic wisdom of the priestess from Mantinea. And far from insisting on the lack of distance and the immediate touching upon, Irigaray enlarges and sets in motion the very border, the very intermediary zone. According to Irigaray what matters in Diotima's speech is the coincidence of Eros's functions as procreation and as a daimon of mediation: Eros *gives birth to mediation*; the offspring and the *ergon* of Eros is the very mean between the lovers; procreation is a rebirth of the one through the other, a passage to immortality in and through one another. Eros, according to Irigaray, becomes a daimon of mediation precisely through this internal fecundity of love, through its continual internal dynamic. Thus from the topography of the self-touching female body in *This Sex Which Is Not One*, Luce Irigaray (1992) turns toward the mystery of "a living, moving border. Changed through contact with your body" (p. 51). This is the mystery of bodies lighted from within, of the erotic in-between as fruitful in itself beyond the ideologies of the carnal or spiritual fecundity.

Irigaray believes that Diotima gives up her vision of the in-between when she introduces the ideology of offspring and procreation. The child, the fruit, the product, be it of the flesh or of the spirit, ascribes a telos to love. Love, Irigaray contends, should have no other telos but itself. In excluding the product from *tokos* and the *ergon* of love, Irigaray differs from Woolf and Kristeva. Nevertheless, she retains and in fact makes more palpable an important node in their reading of Diotima. For Kristeva, Diotima is the agent of mediation that shackles the death drive of the male libido. For Woolf, Diotima is the agent of intoxicating and precarious erotization of the female libido that requires mediation. Irigaray sees Diotima's wisdom precisely in the instance where *tokos* and the in-between coincide. All three accounts converge in their emphasis on the significance of mediation.

THE DEAD BROTHER

According to an anonymous song widely spread throughout the Balkans (in fact, its study inaugurated the establishment of Balkan studies as a distinct field), a wealthy matchmaker comes from far away to ask for the hand of Petkana, the only daughter of the mother of nine sons. The mother is unwilling to let her daughter go to such a distant place. The youngest brother, Lazar, intercedes—the suitor is too prominent, the match too brilliant to be rejected. Petkana has nine brothers; if each of them took a turn once a year to bring her back, or take her mother to her, there would be reunions more than enough. Petkana is wedded and leaves.

Soon after the wedding, the Plague comes with her lists and ledgers—a mysterious deputy of God, whom the bleak Balkan imagination depicts as the supplier of souls on a mass scale for the construction of God's heavenly city. All nine brothers are dead. Left alone, the mother curses her youngest son for the calamitous advice that separated her from her daughter. Tormented by the curses, Lazar entreats God to let him come out of the grave in order to fulfill his promise. The plea is granted. Lazar finds Petkana dancing in the village square with the other young women, and the terrible journey back home begins. Why is he so pale? Why is his hand greenish? Why does he smell of dampness and earth? Elusive, ambiguous answers keep Petkana going. At last the journey is done and Lazar disappears in the churchyard where he has "forgotten something." The daughter faces the mother.

> They embraced alive;
> They let go dead.

Situated within the circuit of the well-forgotten Eleusinian mysteries, how did this grim inversion of the Demeter–Persephone mother–daughter reunion come about? The song offers a glimpse from the obverse side of the emergence of Lévi-Strauss's symbolic, which requires that women, like words, should be things that are exchanged. With its focus on a mother–daughter relationship that regards the brothers as the necessary go-betweens, the song seems to point toward a social contract, a promise that accompanied that emergence—the promise of a return, of a mutuality of mediation. The anonymous authors of the song knew that the promise was not kept. They inserted, in the place of the failure, the mysterious agency of the Plague with her complicity in an ideality that feeds on corpses.

6

Woolf's Final Answer

In women's writing, language seems to be seen from a foreign land; is it seen from the point of view of an asymbolic, spastic body? Virginia Woolf describes suspended states, subtle sensations and, above all, colours— green, blue—, but she does not dissect language as Joyce does. Estranged from language, women are visionaries, dancers who suffer as they speak.
[Kristeva 1981, p. 166]

SARA COLERIDGE'S DOTS

As early as *The Voyage Out*, Woolf's character Terence Hewet recounts his dream of writing a novel about silence. The difficulty of writing a novel about silence is, Hewet contends, immense. Silence . . . Which silence? Cosmic silence, the shivering of atoms beyond the dimensions where sound can vibrate? Or silence as an interruption of speech, as the suffocation of potential voices? Or silence as inarticulateness, as noise? While Hewet's project is somewhat vaguely described as concerned with what people do not say (do not want to say? cannot say?), *The Voyage Out* itself is pursuing its own speechless agenda. As Woolf explains in a letter to Lytton Strachey, her novel had to "give a feeling of the tumult of life, as various and disorderly as possible, which should be cut short for a moment by the death, and go on again" (Woolf 1912–1922, p. 82). Situated on the far sides of language as they are, both tumult and its cutting short involve difficulties of which Woolf is as acutely aware as her character Hewet. "Do you think it is impossible to get this sort of effect in a novel;—is the result bound to be too scattered to be intelligible?" (p. 82).

In her subsequent work, Woolf persists in her efforts to solve the immense difficulty of writing about silence, risking to remain, as she fears in the letter, misunderstood. As J. Graham (1990) remarks in connection with *Between the Acts*, it is perhaps what he terms the "interval" in Woolf's writing that may explain the wide diversity of critical interpretation and judgment—and, indeed, of critical incomprehension—that surrounds Woolf's last novel. According to Shari Benstock (1991), Woolf's texts have to be read letter by letter and ellipsis by ellipses. The challenge that Woolf confronts as early as *The Voyage Out* and that continues to present a challenge to her readers seems to involve the problem of heeding an alternative code, a silent code—a writing in which the gaps are read.

Does it mean that Woolf writes "as if silence were of the same order as the readable, the same order as words on the page" (Laurence 1991, p. 5)? Would not such a hypothesis place us, as readers, on the side of Septimus Smith for whom "sounds made harmonies with premeditation; the spaces between them were as significant as the sounds" (Woolf 1925a, p. 24)—on the side, that is, of what Daniel Ferrer (1990) has called the "madness" of Woolf's language? Whatever the stakes, Woolf's preoccupation with the spaces between sounds and with, so to speak, the notation and the hieroglyphics of these spaces is so persistent that her work cannot be adequately approached if it is approached only in terms of its language. It has to be approached in its dual positioning "between language and silence." According to Howard Harper (1982), who wrote a book with this title, this positioning sets the stage for Woolf's mythical struggles with the ineffable; it exemplifies the paradigmatic human effort to wrestle meaning from the protean phenomenal world and to make the silence speak. Rachel Bowlby (1988) on the other hand, makes a few interesting "points or dots" on Woolf's use of the dotted line as a "line that is not joined up, that shows up its gaps" (p. 164). Bowlby interprets this intrusive showing up of the gaps within the sentence as a critique of language and as a mode of feminist interrogation of the masculine rules of writing.

There is, therefore, Kristeva's question as to what Woolf does to and with language, but there is also the question what she does to and with silence, with the "sudden shocks," as she herself puts it (Woolf 1985, p. 72). The silence somehow has not remained on the side of the spastic body but has found its way into Woolf's writing. How does Woolf "read silence" (Laurence 1991)? Is her oeuvre exemplifying an "aesthetic of disjunction" (Ruotolo 1986)? Does she seek, as Patricia Laurence (1991) believes, to "express silence, its nature, its meanings, and its uses" (p. 5)? Or does she "take up a position with relation to the ultimate limits of discourse, madness, and death," as Ferrer's (1990, p. 142) study contends? Does Woolf make silence speak, as Harper would have it, or does she silence the (male) order of speaking, as Bowlby insists? Or does she, perhaps, rotate different possibilities which, as J. Hillis Miller (1982) maintains in *Fiction and Repetition*, she cannot master for they allow no mastery?

In a remarkable late essay on Sara Coleridge, contemporaneous with the writing of *Between the Acts*, Woolf seems to be tackling precisely these questions. The essay is presented as a gloss on the three rows of dots with which, after an interrupted sentence, Sara Coleridge ended her twenty-six page autobiographical fragment. Woolf's essay gives in to the temptation to fill in and read Sara Coleridge's dots, developing the fragment into a life story and providing an explanation for the never-finished autobiography (silence is wrestled with). On the other hand, however, in the explanation offered by Woolf, the abundant dots in Sara Coleridge's autobiography are interpreted as a sort of ascesis, an abstention from finishing, dictated by an awareness of the false conclusiveness that writing demands. Sara Coleridge's life, "very still but always in motion" (Woolf 1942, p. 73), is compressed by Woolf in a few breathlessly short moments between the memory of little Sara's separation from her mother, which marks the ambiguous advent of her father, and the interruption by cancer of her never finished rounds of writing and erasing. Sara Coleridge's dots thus become a commentary on what she herself saw as a propensity of writing to "complete incompletely" (pp. 76, 77). Covering separations and interruptions, writing remains incomplete precisely through its pretense at completion. The dots are hence allowed to invade Woolf's own discussion of her unfinished subject (silence questions language and takes up a position in relation to the ultimate limits of discourse).

In one neat stroke, the essay on Sara Coleridge demonstrates that both the reading of silence and the critique of language have relevance for understanding Woolf's use of the spaces between sounds. "But still . . . dots intervene" (Woolf 1942, p. 73). No matter whether language fights silence, or is critically exposed by it, the focus remains on language—on its power in need of exertion, or its limitations in need of precarious exposure and revision. Woolf's fondness for the line that shows up its gaps, on the other hand, seems frequently to have been dictated by the intention neither to enunciate the gaps, nor to utilize them as an instrument of critique, but to . . . , and this is a point at which we may glance again briefly at the essay on Sara Coleridge. It is presented as an answer and an addition to Sara

Coleridge's biography written by Leslie Griggs "exhaustively, sympatheti-cally; but still . . ." Dots intervene. It is the dots that Woolf's essay wants to append; through its very exhaustiveness, Grigg's biography has completed incompletely and Woolf's short piece offers to complete this incompletion by adding . . .

The dots. Woolf's essay reads and fills in Sara Coleridge's dots in order to be read as—emptied out into—. . . It effects a double movement that transforms the dots into words and returns the words into the dots. Unwrites them. One cannot help remarking that through this procedure Woolf of-fers a solution, however disturbing, to the strange spaces of silence that she points out as characteristic of the history of female achievement—to the absence of tradition of the mothers. The essay reads absence, the strange spaces of silence—Sara Coleridge's dots. Yet it reads them without com-pleting them, without exhausting them as Sara Coleridges's biographer does. It constitutes itself and requires to be read as a (necessarily discontinuous) continuation of the dots. Of silence and incompletion. In this way, like the inhabitants of Pointz Hall in *Between the Acts*, Woolf's work situates itself as the inheritor of a dual ancestry. On the one hand there is the pic-ture of the ancestor: the man with a big name, the talk-producer, the pro-prietor with the rein in his hand. On the other hand there is the lady who is not an ancestress but a picture: offering an alternative ancestry of ano-nymity, silence, and indifference to property.

Such an ancestry—where the father is known, and the mother is not—necessitates an approach to Woolf's work from the viewpoint of silences and ellipses, interruptions and pauses. That is, from the viewpoint of the "acts of interval" (Graham), the acts "between the acts," the entre-acts. And yet how can the pause be described in its own act, without being turned into speech, how can one keep in mind that the mad language of Woolf insists simultaneously on writing and its absence? Before turning to the inheritance of ellipses and interruptions, to the genealogy of the interval, certain clarifications are necessary.

A SILENCE THAT KILLS AND A SILENCE THAT CALLS

Woolf is ambivalent toward language (Naremore 1973), but she is no less ambivalent toward silence. There is the angel of silence, stifling the indi-vidual woman's voice; there are the strange spaces of silence that mark women's achievements with a kind of historical stammer. This is the silence that kills and, subsequently, the silence that has to be killed by doing what Martin Luther did to chase away the devil: by flinging an inkpot at the intruder.

In an entry from her *Diary*, however, Woolf seems to revive Hewet's project for a novel about what people do not say and professes to be "very little persuaded of the truth of anything—what I say, what people say—always to follow, blindly, instinctively with a sense of leaping over a precipice—the call of—the call of—now, if I write *The Moths* [the working title of *The Waves*] I must come to terms with these mystical feelings" (Woolf 1953, pp. 136–137).

Writing is seen as following the call of—a syntactic fracture, an interruption that is clasping at words as at a life buoy. An earlier entry from the time of Woolf's work on *To the Lighthouse* suggests that the hiatus was caused by a fin passing far out. "One sees a fin passing far out. What image can I reach to convey what I mean?" (Woolf 1953, p. 104). The fin, erasing the replete meaningfulness of the lighthouse, stamps the waters with a metaphysical dash: a failure of language, a rupture, a break. This mystical pause is a call for—what? An image, a narrative, a meaning? Something to render it?

Another syntactic—and mystical—rupture introduces Woolf's description of her illnesses. Once again, the rupture promises a moth. "I believe these illnesses are in my case—how shall I express it—partly mystical." The mind totally shuts itself up; it refuses to go on registering impressions; it becomes chrysalis. Then suddenly a change comes, something springs, "and this is I believe the moth shaking its wings in me. I then begin to make up my story whatever it is" (Woolf 1953, pp. 151–152).

A silence that kills; a silence that calls; a silence that shuts itself up like a chrysalis in which new stories shake their wings. One turns to writing—flings the ink pot at the angel of silence—by turning to a lacuna where speech falters. "But by writing I don't reach anything." (Woolf 1953, p. 104). How is it to be reached, then? Writing is good enough for killing the silence, yet it is not sufficient for answering its call.

THE MOTH AND PRESIDENT KRUGER

Unwriting would be the process that turns words into Sara Coleridge's dots, yet only through a reversal that reads the dots. In what follows, I shall focus on Woolf's hieroglyphics of silence rendered as interruption: as the interruption of syntax, the interruption of the story (and hence of illusion, of fiction-making), and the interruption of interpretation. Woolf's earliest consistent codification of silence appears in "An Unwritten Novel." In it, Woolf's silent code—her "unwriting"—operates as a disruptive agent that questions the naive self-confidence of the story, and never allows it to forget itself into life. This disruptive agent, although presupposing and demanding fictionality as a condition for its own articulation, is manifested only as a suspension of fiction. It is articulated as a hiatus, a pause, a stammering of speech, a gap between words; it takes the form of a dash, a question mark, a breaking off of syntax, of stylistic coherence, or of the story itself. It is the unwritten in the written as the paradox of the title shows.

The story about Miss Marsh—a name that in itself indicates the treacherous grounds of the fictional endeavor—evolves out of the observation of a passenger in a train. It begins as an attempt at imaginative identification of the narrator with the "twitch" and the "rub" of the woman whom she wants to describe: a curious gesture of appropriation that ultimately confounds the problem as to where the abrupt and angular movements originate. The twitching woman is presented by the narrator as a woman who "looks at life" and it is this relentless looking, presumably, that urges her incessantly to rub the window and induces an irresistible twitch in her. The twitch—denying all hope and discounting all illusion, that is, marking some unspeakable revelation—constantly interrupts the narrator's story and forces her, in her turn, to look at her model and not give in to illusion. The twitch becomes, in this way, an analogue for the narrative procedure; the persistent breaking up of the story—like the woman's breaking of an eggshell into the fragments of a puzzling map—can claim to be a supermimetic act that follows its twitching model. The story about Miss Marsh is constantly interrupted (it "twitches") and is constantly questioned as to its truthfulness (the seemingly transparent windows are "rubbed").

We could say that the story is interrupted by the very questioning—that the rubbing causes the twitching. Again and again the narrator stops her narrative in order to compare Miss Marsh to the woman opposite her and thus to confirm the reliability of her own approach. Instead of providing confirmation, however, these shifts emphasize the fits and starts of a story being made up, the "here's a jerk" (Woolf 1944, p. 20) of an abrupt change of perspective, which seems to repeat the erratic movement of the train rather than any other exigency.

Whatever the origin of the fits and twitches, things keep disappearing in them. What collapses in the sudden rifts is usually some fundamental referent—God, life, or the human soul—toward which the story inadvertently veers only to stumble upon it and crack. In what seems to be the central passage of "An Unwritten Novel" the moth (Woolf's habitual image of the soul, but also of the story-telling capacity that shakes its wings in the mystical chrysalis) is consistently described in terms of breaking and fragmentation. It appears in "a break—a division" of the human eye; the syntax of the passage that follows is indented by "breaks and divisions" and leads to a sentence never finished after the mention of "immortality" (Woolf 1944, p. 20). "Just as you've seen him, felt him, someone interrupts" (p. 19)—this time the interruption refers to the seeing of President Kruger, that is, Miss Marsh's God. The mentioning of President Kruger invariably leads to a temporary paralysis of language, and a virtual breaking off of the sentence. It is obviously in the nature of God to be seen and felt as an interruption. But—ironically or not—this seems to be in the nature of all ontological conjectures.

Like life, for example. "Life's what you see in people's eyes; life is what they learn, and having learnt it, never, though they seek to hide it, cease to be aware of—what?" (p. 14). The awareness is interrupted by—what? By a dash, an interrogative pronoun, a question mark: by a question. In the next sentence the question is answered by a more colloquial, casual, unspecific, and somewhat anticlimactic repetition ("that life's like that," that is, life is what they learn and they never cease to be aware of what they learn). The answer introduces a circularity, a tautology of "they know what they know." What we get is that they never cease to be aware of what they are aware of—with an interrogative pause between awareness and—awareness. The answer to the question about life has been silenced; it has, in fact, remained in the question itself, in the interrogative breaking off of the text, in the interruption.

The broken syntax of this passage is repeated and magnified in the breaking off of the story of Miss Marsh. With the appearance of the unlooked-for son, not only the fiction of the childless Miss Marsh but also the twitching observation (now clearly a fiction, too) of the unhappy woman in the train, as well as the "here's a jerk" of the narrator's procedure, have to renounce their claims for mimetic precision. At the sight of this unforeseen disaster, the story can do nothing but stop! It reverts into a turmoil of dashes, dots, question marks, and unfinished sentences. Life is manifested as a narrative catastrophe, as bareness ("life's bare as bone"), as paralysis of speech, as interruption of the fictional enterprise.

It is noteworthy, however, that this final rupture is easily overcome. One might expect it to put an end to the story-telling; and yet the narrator survives the disaster; on she goes integrating the interruption into a new fictional beginning; into a new series of questions. "Who are you? Why do you walk down the street?"—exactly the kind of questions that the story of Miss Marsh was designed to answer. The gap, the breach of fictionality has the effect of setting in motion a further fictional endeavor; new stories shake their wings in it.

Thus, from fiction to fiction, the narrator knows what she knows, and she tells what she tells. But there is a dash between knowing and—knowing, between telling and—telling. In her later work, Woolf never quite loses sight of the discovery she makes in "An Unwritten Novel." In *The Waves*, the novel that, as mentioned earlier, was written as an answer to the call of a mystical gap, Woolf attempts to embody interruption in the heavy and solid figure of Percival. Percival is the complete human being who never speaks, who invariably suspends the stories of Bernard (Percival's fiction-producing antipode) by his absolute presence, and for whom not a sheet of paper lies between him and the sun. For Bernard, the coiner of phrases, Percival is "what cannot be accounted for, what turns symmetry to nonsense. . . . The little apparatus of observation is unhinged" (Woolf 1931, p. 243). The notation of rupture—of the unhinging of the apparatus of observation that underlies Bernard's dream of broken, inarticulate words—thus seems to imprint a mark on the wall. It is a stumbling over the real, which both suspends and urges on story-telling. It is in *Between the Acts*, however, that the aesthetic of disjunction surfaces once again in the title and pervasively employs silence to make its problematic contribution to talk.

THE UR-INTERRUPTION

Is not the moth, Woolf's habitual image of the soul and of her own creativity, is not this emblem of her art the fragment of an interrupted word, the word for moth-er? The final interruption in "An Unwritten Novel" is brought about by the reunification of a mother with her son. Fragmentation thus seems to remain on the side of story-telling and the gap that disjoins and urges the story on becomes the intimation of a totality that unhinges the apparatus of observation because it is situated in a world without interruption, without a sheet of paper to separate it from the sun. While the narrator contemplates the puzzle of the fragmented egg shell, Miss Marsh eats the egg whole. Interruption, then, curiously delivers a message from a world without interruption.

It is questionable whether this first intimation persists beyond "An Unwritten Novel." The split between Septimus and Clarissa in *Mrs. Dalloway*, and the emergence of Lily Briscoe's vision out of the death of Mrs. Ramsay hint at other possibilities. Percival, the complete human being, is dead for a good part of the novel. In "A Sketch of the Past" Woolf (1985) describes as a sudden shock the brutal "token of some real thing behind appearances" (p. 72), which is all but murderous. Yet the sudden shock also bestows the "moments of being," the moments when one is truly alive. The reality of the real thing behind it, however, seems to be of a strange nature since in a single sentence Woolf states that the shock *is* the token of the real thing, and that she *makes* it real by putting it into words. What emerges in this sentence is the paradox of concepts apprehended, like Kristeva's chora, through difficult reasoning: lost as soon as they are posited but nonexistent without this positing. Hence the thing *is* and I *make* it, and, Woolf adds, "it is only through putting it into words that I make it whole" (Woolf 1985, p. 72). The words hence make the thing *and* cover the rift that this thing opened.

In a much discussed crisis in *Between the Acts*, the wind blows gaps between the words of Miss La Trobe's actors and she, paralyzed with the failure of illusion, murmurs "this is death" (Woolf 1941, p. 99). As I shall try to emphasize later on, no interruption in Woolf's last novel is ever that final. It is bridged in this instance, too, by the interference of the cows who fill the gap with their howling. The howl—alluding simultaneously to the mother-goddess and to erotic frenzy—is initiated by a cow who has lost her calf. The gap is hence bridged by a separation, rather than a reunion, the primary separation between mother and child. One should note the paradoxical nature of this bridging that points toward an ultimate breach. Are we offered a glimpse, then, of the first separation as the Ur-interruption with unity only a linguistic mirage? Could the sudden shock be a token of terrifying splitting, could the real thing behind appearances be a—gap?

The question should better remain suspended since one of the persistent effects of interruption in *Between the Acts* is to undercut any definitive statement about the novel, not because of some failure in Woolf's writing, or because of some inalterable condition of reading, but because of a certain diabolic strategy operating throughout the text. And yet, before proceeding with Woolf's baffling employment of interruption in *Between the Acts*, some consideration of the question becomes unavoidable. What is there, behind the gaps, behind the spasms of speech? Is there a hidden presence—God, life, the human soul, the complete human being, the real thing, or whatever it might be? Or is something really missing and the gap is the thing? If we accept the second possibility, what would be the proper work of the writer? To make the gap appear, or to weave a veil over the emptiness? J. Hillis Miller (1982) asks all these questions and concludes that Woolf's work "affirms now one possibility, now another, now all three at once, in a rotation which Woolf does not master and could not master, since each possibility contains the others and calls them up" (p. 230). Since no possibility can be chosen, the meaning of the gap cannot be fixed, hence the challenge that *Between the Acts* presents to the reader is exemplary for a perennial condition of reading.

"Speaking beings . . . demand a break, a renunciation, an unease at their foundations" (Kristeva 1989, p. 42). Against the background of linguistic theory and language learning, Kristeva places emptiness at the root of the human psyche and at the beginnings of the symbolic function. As the first and most fragile screen of the primeval separation of an ego that is not yet an ego from an object that is not yet an object, emptiness is the treacherous surface of Narcissus's pool, a quivering shield against a hidden presence that had better remain hidden. Woolf's "A Sketch of the Past" offers a late rationalization of the boon of the "sudden shocks," the deadly reminders of the thing behind appearances, that demand to be put into words. The putting into words is a buffer against the murderous power of the thing, yet it is only the shocks that bestow the "moments of being." It is only through the shocks that the speaking subject comes to life. From that point of view, interruption and the enhancement of the spaces between the sounds would be the reintroduction of the earliest and most fragile defense against the thing, threatening, but in a creative manner, protecting, but in the most precarious way. For what might break the surface of the mirror—rise up and make the pool of Narcissus turgid—is the abject and, with it, chaos, the destruction of the possibility for any distinction or trace. But also—to stress this point once again— the demand for a new word, a new rhythm, and a new language, which arises with the triggering of an archaic, maternal tongue, and through which art "challenges the universe of established values, pokes fun at them" (Kristeva 1987b, p. 127). We might very well be witnessing this unsettling of Narcissus's pool with Miss La Trobe when, in a transformation of all mirrors and ponds that appear before that, "words without meaning—wonderful words" rise up from the "fertile mud" (Woolf 1941, p. 147).

We seem to get an ironic glimpse of the same process in "An Unwritten Novel" where prayers emerge from waters swirling with monsters, and a starker version of it in *Mrs. Dalloway*, where Septimus observes the "gradual drawing together of everything to one center before his eyes, as if some horror had come almost to the surface and was about to burst into flames" (Woolf 1925a, p. 16). Between the fire and the monsters of the deep (we already discussed this "choice of evils" in the context of abjection and terrorism), the problem would seem to be not so much a problem of rotating or mastering certain indeterminate possibilities but rather of daring to confront the choices in their capacity to kill, or renovate the story. In its very perilousness, the mystical gap is productive.

FREEDOM FROM OLD LOYALTIES

There are aspects to the mystical gap, however, that need not take us to the Ur-interruption or that, at the very least, have been deliberately reformulated in Woolf's later work. "Not an ancestress," says Mrs. Swithin about the lady who is a picture and who leads into the heart of silence. "But we claim her because we've known her—O, ever so many years" (Woolf 1941, p. 52) The possibility of claiming silence for ancestry offers an answer to the unresolved question of *A Room of One's Own*, concerning the tradition of the mothers. A tradition does not have to begin with existent texts, it may—and perhaps far more adequately—begin with nonexistent ones (Sara Coleridge's dots).

Claiming silence and uncertainty as an ancestry, moreover, can hardly come as a surprise for Occidental culture, which has repeatedly claimed such beginnings and constituted itself through pseudo-relations. Socrates, of course, is paradigmatic, but there is also the problem of Plato's unwritten doctrine, there is the lure of Aristotle's *Poetics*, a broken and fragmentary text based probably on the notes for his lectures. Such figures have recurred, foregrounding rather than concealing the play of presence and absence, and epitomizing the situation of any text whose completion is always only apparent. Thus Schleiermacher, the father of scientific hermeneutics, that is, of the very problem of approaching the past as text, made a demonstration of his method in an attempt to reconstitute the true Socratic teaching, that is, a nontext. Yet Schleiermacher's method itself was left in a fragmentary form, for the latecomers to fill in. Providing a continuation for the dots would thus seem to be a perennial cultural temptation. In the figure of

Saussure (and Lacan, and Foucault's late unfinished projects), our times, so obsessively documented, have repeated the fascination with the fragmented word, the word carried away by the wind the way the songs of La Trobe's actors are carried away—the word that we, the latecomers, have to write down in the name of those that precede us.

Except that, according to the radical leanings of Woolf's late works, there should be no name in the name of which to write. *Between the Acts* was written immediately after *Three Guineas* and more than ten years after *A Room of One's Own*. As mentioned earlier, although they share a common framework of fire and its deferral, the distance separating *Three Guineas* from *A Room of One's Own* is in many respects so great that they present two drastically opposed solutions to the problems of woman, writing, inheritance, futurity, fame, property, or indeed, anything. The solution in *A Room of One's Own* is to think back through the mothers. Accept the great tradition (Shakespeare, Coleridge): it is not all-male, it is androgynous. Own a room. Write books. The solution in *Three Guineas*, to begin with, much more ruthlessly states its extreme setting. The Thames marks the one extreme. "Rags. Petrol. Matches."—marks the other extreme. If the meditation in *A Room of One's Own* begins by the river, in *Three Guineas* it is repeatedly positioned on a bridge. Burn the library, or plunge off the bridge? With a lucidity, that has made Woolf's later feminist book by far the less popular, Woolf follows the logic of extremism to wherever it takes her: burning or drowning, terrorism or suicide. Turning to a nameless genealogy comes as a deferral of such extremes. Thus in spite my own narrative of the ellipses characterizing the classical inheritance (a ruin-as-form) and in spite of Woolf's own emphasis on the impossibility of knowing Greek, the quasi-kinship with the ancient world established by Occidental culture is regarded by Woolf as the choice of an authored past, of the talk-producing ancestor with the big name. This choice is made at the expense of Anon—the local nameless predecessors. The writer facing the historical choice that grafted the beginning of the new European literatures was in a situation somewhat analogous to the situation of the woman writer in search of her mothers: ignoring Anon, he confronted "his lack of intellectual ancestry" (Silver 1979, p. 385).

For Woolf "the death of the author" means an author who "is not distinct from [the] book" (Silver 1979, p. 385). Her turn toward anonymity offers a historical perspective that circumscribes authorship within its legitimate boundaries. The question persists, however, as to whether Woolf's late choice of a nameless lineage, her discovery of the maternal heritage through anonymity and silence, should not be regarded as part of a suicidal teleology behind which we have to read the story of her death. Is Woolf's attempt to position art in a genealogy of anonymity and silence the sign of a self-deceived movement toward dissolution, of a relinquishment of the symbolic hold on life? Is the placing of cogitation between fire and water dictated by an enticement, rather than a knowledgeable deferral? Does the curtain in the end of *Between the Acts* rise on nothing—"on the unnameable, madness, death" (Ferrer 1990, p. 106).

SOMEONE ALWAYS TAKES THE FLOOR

Nothing is ever left to take its own course in *Between the Acts*. Lucy's reading is interrupted by the maid; Bartholomew's nap, by Isa's entering the room; the family dinner, by unexpected guests; the beginning of the pageant, by latecomers. Communication as a rule fails because nobody answers, or an answer comes where it is not asked; the "I remember . . ." is as frequently pronounced, as it is interrupted; in any case, what people remember turns out to be a string of trifling or unintelligible fragments. Isa's desire for the man in gray is interrupted by his wife, by the ordering of fish for dinner, by the crowds at the pageant, by the Victorian prayer, by the activity of the "hindquarters of the donkey, represented by Albert the idiot" (Woolf 1941, p. 119). Miss La Trobe's pageant, torn as it is by gaps and rifts of all sorts, is played against the background of a chorus of villagers whose words are systematically carried away by the wind. All these interruptions, whose listing and classification might exceed the length of the novel, occur against the background of the fracturing of English literary history that La Trobe's parodic pageant presents, and of the threat of total destruction, posed by the impending war.

And yet, although *Between the Acts* unfolds the fragmented story of a particularized world against the background of total destruction, there is, in the novel, a pronounced intolerance toward pauses and blanks. Sometimes the intolerance is dictated by embarrassment and a fear of silence—it is not polite not to talk. Most often, however, and much more strikingly, any interruption is used as an opportunity for another voice to assert itself. In the very beginning of the novel, when Mrs. Haines suspends the conversation with a silly remark, a cow coughs, prefiguring a whole series of similar intrusions. Throughout the whole novel, in and out of the pageant, nature seems on the alert to fill any interval that the human world provides. The audience and the landscape fill the crevasses of Miss La Trobe's pageant. However desperate Miss La Trobe might be about the interval, which sends the audience to have tea, the interval provides an opportunity for Manresa, the "wild child of nature," who is (so much about wildness and nature) staging each of her movements, to set forth her own acting. The interval is not an interruption of the pageant as Cobbet of Cobbs Corner, who has seen life both in the East and in the West, very well knows; there is always an agency that utilizes the break. If not another voice, then the unsaid fills the gaps of the said; silence makes "its contribution to talk" "as plainly as words could say it" (Woolf 1941, pp. 39, 81). Accomplishing the dream project of Woolf's first novel, there is a consistent tendency in *Between the Acts* toward perforating the spoken dialogue with an unspoken one.

The interruption, therefore, functions as a clearing for the reverberation of another voice, or for the initiative of another agent. Between the acts there are other acts.

UP THE MONKEY-PUZZLE TREE

This tendency for every sequence or coherence to be interrupted is especially true with respect to the interpretations that the novel readily provides for its own reading, as well as with respect to the pageant that duplicates the novel's procedures. With its strategies, which have been likened to the Möbius strip and which undermine all divisions between reality and fiction, nature and civilization, and with its confusing dispersal of perspectives that often cannot be clearly localized with this or that character, the novel turns into a real interpretive trap. One of the participants in a discussion dedicated to Woolf's centenary complains about *Between the Acts* being "so *knowing*" (Warner 1984, p. 164). The complaint does not seem to need argumentation nowadays after so many interpretations had to face the diabolic propensity of the novel to foresee them, include them in its own narrative, and in the long run deride them. It is noteworthy, however, that the initial grievances about the novel concern its lack of unity and design, its chaotic lack of control. This was ascribed to Woolf's deepening psychological crisis, and to the fact that she did not succeed in finishing her work. It is quite obvious today that the constantly displaced perspective, the interruptions, and the sketchy rendering of the characters speak of a relentless hold that always gives the floor to the pervasive knowingness of the text. After a life of painful confrontations with her critics, Woolf finally had her revenge.

Thus, after the pageant, Mr. Streatfield, the pastor, appears on a soap box. The last scene in the pageant was announced as "The present. Ourselves" and consists of numerous mirrors turned by the actors toward the audience. The novel, too—a point to which we will return—ends with a similar mirror, a similar gaping turned toward us. Confused, the pastor foreshadows our shocked questioning: what message (he is, of course, interrupted several times even before starting to speak) does the pageant convey? Very aptly, he begins a sermon on unity. This most pertinent critical response to the pageant is discontinued at least three times: the military aeroplanes cut in two the word op-portunity (what about war?); contemplating the village idiot, Mr. Streatfield loses the thread of his discourse (united with him, too?); and finally the desire to smoke overcomes his desire to speak (Can *this* be integrated? The question is with us still.). Mr. Streatfield's search for the message is thus no more successful than his other search: Who is responsible for all this? Whom to thank? To whom at the end there shall be an invocation? Is there no one?

Because of the blurring of the distinction between reality and illusion, Mr. Streatfield's question concerns the pageant but also the world as well as the novel itself—taking us in this way to the dispersal of the author's agency, but also to the impossibility of locating the one responsible for a world in the shadow of a new war. The question receives no answer—or rather, it receives several incompatible answers. Maybe no one is responsible. Or maybe nature ("the swish of the trees; the gulp of a cow; even the skim of the swallows over the grass"). Then a scuffle is heard behind the bush where Miss La Trobe's place is; a scratching of the gramophone's needle and a chuff, chuff, chuff. So maybe the stammering of history, the broken gramophone of a deadly repetitiveness (such a metaphor appears also in *Three Guineas*). Or is Miss La Trobe responsible? After the scratching a word finally emerges from the gramophone—God—God is responsible!—a new interruption and the audience rises to their feet—save the king.

It seems as though, teasing and frustrating the desires of Etty Springett who "liked to leave a theatre knowing exactly what was meant" (Woolf 1941, p. 115), the novel is engaged in a process that can be derived from its acts of interval in their specific deployment as interruption of "what is meant." Through the joint effect of rupture and the dispersal of the narrative voice, where it is not at all clear who is to be made responsible or thanked, each attempt at rationalization (and there are numerous such attempts within the novel itself) is broken off; explanations are discontinued; as demonstrated in the case of Mr. Streatfield, the novel reshuffles and rearranges itself with the quite definite goal of suspending the interpretations that it could generate. The novel, consequently, presents us with a sustained hermeneutical stammer. It might very well be described as "full of wanton . . . jokes" as Frank Kermode, the literary critic, does (Warner 1984, p. 165), who has as much right to say so as Ferrer, who sees it as taking us to the limits of madness and death. What has to be added, however, is the necessary qualification that the jokes have a definite addressee and a precision that forges, within the text, a sort of puzzle, a critical puzzle, or a puzzle for critics—and, perhaps, if we have in mind the indefatigable Mr. Page who sedulously and condescendingly illuminates Miss La Trobe's meanings—a monkey puzzle, too.

The view of the novel as a monkey puzzle is, of course, undercut by it. It is a view that is procured through the position of Cobbet of Cobbs Corner, an angular view, a somewhat outsider's view since Cobbet is a newcomer who has seen life both in the East and in the West, who notices no interruption in the movement of the pageant from the stage of acting to the stage of eating, and for whom art is no excuse for forgetting to water his plants. It is he who, alone under the monkey-puzzle tree, asks: "What was in her mind, eh? What lay behind, eh? What made her indue the antique with this glamour—this sham lure, and set 'em climbing, climbing, climbing up the monkey puzzle tree?" Yet it is after looking at him that Miss La Trobe is struck by the thought that "she hadn't made them see. It was a failure, another damned failure!" (Woolf 1941, pp. 71, 72).

We have to assume that she is also wrong.

WORDS WITHOUT MEANING

After the pageant, in the pub, nodding over her glass, Miss La Trobe hears there rise above the fertile mud, above the nondescript sources of creation, the first words of her "play behind the play." The words she hears are notoriously the words that Isa and Giles speak beyond the finale of *Between the Acts*. This finale takes the protagonists to the "night before roads were made, or houses" (Woolf 1941, p. 152). A primal scene is hence revealed among the caves and rocks of this ancient night, where a woman and a man confront each other on the verge of fighting and embracing. Yet, while the novel lasts, they neither fight nor embrace. They speak—but they do not speak either, for the last sentences of the novel are "The curtain rose. They spoke."

What did they speak? Marked as it is by ruptures and breaks, in its very end the novel takes us to a rift. This rift opens up into a world that is never completed; it completes the novel by adding to it incompletion. The novel is thus posited as an inheritor to Sara Coleridge's lines of dots and beyond them to an ancestry that can be claimed even if it is silent. This rift is from such a point of view an opening of space into an oscillation of time. It takes us back to the beginning of humanity (the "night before roads were made"), back to the beginning of the novel ("it was a summer's night and they were talking . . ."), and back to an ancestry of incompletion. Yet it also takes us forward, inviting another voice to assert itself. This voice, invoked to reverberate after the last words, is prepared by the porous texture of the novel, by the persistent insertion of alternative agencies in any and every interval, by the shifting perspective, by the undermining of each interpretation. Did Woolf intend to save the world through her novel? In "Thoughts on Peace in an Air Raid" Woolf (1942) exhorts the necessity to "think peace into existence" (p. 154). The final blank of *Between the Acts* speaks the next story into existence, the unend of narrating. It is as if Woolf wanted to create a novel that—without going back to its beginning, without closing its cycle as with James Joyce's *Finnegan's Wake*—never ends. Completed through its incompletion, it insists upon the endlessness of the story. Since it insists also upon the collapsing differentiation between reality and fiction—it insists upon the unend of the world. By not completing incompletely—opening, instead, into a blank similar to Sara Coleridge's dots—the novel cannot be finished. It will continue forever, opening the space for the next voice, the voice that comes later, ourselves. It would mean that the sudden rift in the finale, in agreement with the novel's overall punctuated stylistic, does not "raise the curtain on nothingness" but rather on whatever is. It cannot be interpreted because it is the world. And may be precisely in its aspect of a perpetuum mobile the novel becomes a prelude to Woolf's suicide. "There is no need to go on writing since I wrote a novel that by itself can go on writing the world into existence." There is, indeed, something awesome about this masterful joke. Here you are the word, here you are the world. Be! Write! Chuff-chuff, scratch-scratch. But who is responsible for all this? To whom at the end shall there be an invocation? And she fills her pockets with stones but not before this maternal gesture that allows us to be.

References

Adorno, T. W. (1982). Trying to understand *Endgame*. *New German Critique* 26 (Spring–Summer): 119–150.

Aeschylus. (1970). *The Enmenides*, tr. H. Lloyd-Jones. Englewood Cliffs, NJ: Prentice-Hall.

Agamben, G. (1999). *The End of the Poem: Studies in Poetics*. Stanford, CA: Stanford University Press.

Angelova, E. (1992). Death and significance: on the figure of allegory in Benjamin's *The Origin of German Tragic Drama* (unpublished manuscript).

Auerbach, E. (1948). *Mimesis: The Representation of Reality in Western Literature*. Princeton, NJ: Princeton University Press, 1953.

Barrett, M. (1999). *Imagination in Theory: Essays on Writing and Culture*. Cambridge: Polity Press.

Beauvoir, S. (1949). *The Second Sex*, tr. H. M. Parshley. New York: The Modern Library, 1968.

Benhabib, S. (1992). *Situating the Self: Gender, Community and Postmodernism in Contemporary Ethics*. New York: Routledge.

Benjamin, W. (1977). *The Origin of German Tragic Drama*. tr. J. Osborne. London: NLB.

Benstock, S. (1991). *Textualizing the Feminine: On the Limits of Genre*. Norman, OK: University of Oklahoma Press.

Bloom, H. (1973). *The Anxiety of Influence: A Theory of Poetry*. New York: Oxford University Press.

Bollack, T., and Wismann, H. (1972). *Hérachte on la séparation*. Paris: Minuit.

Borges, J. L. (1985). *Fictions*. London: John Calder.

Bowlby, R. (1988). *Virginia Woolf: Feminist Destinations*. Oxford: Basil Blackwell.

Brodskii, I. (1987). *Uraniia*. Ann Arbor, MI: Ardis.

Butler, J. (1990). *Gender Trouble: Feminism and the Subversion of Identity*. New York: Routledge.

———— (1993). *Bodies that Matter: On the Discursive Limits of "Sex."* New York: Routledge.

———— (1997). *The Psychic Life of Power: Theories in Subjection*. Stanford: Stanford University Press.

Chasseguet-Smirgel, J. (1989). *Sexuality and Mind: The Role of the Father and the Mother in the Psyche*. London: Karnac.

Cixous, H. (1975). Sorties. In *The Newly Born Woman*, ed. H. Cixous, and C. Clément, tr. B. Wing, pp. 63–132. Minneapolis, MN: University of Minnesota Press, 1986.

Cornford, F. M. (1950). *The Unwritten Philosophy and Other Essays*. Cambridge: Cambridge University Press.

———— (1956). *Plato's Cosmology. The "Timaeus" of Plato Translated with a Running Commentary*. London: Routledge & Kegan Paul.

Eckermann, J. (1930). *Conversations of Goethe with Eckermann*, tr. J. Oxenford. London: J. M. Dent.

Ehlers, B. (1966). *Eine vorplatonische Deutung des sokratischen Eros: Der Dialog Aspasia des Sokratikers Aischines*. München: C. H. Beck'sche Verlagsbuchhandlung.

Fairfield, S. (1995). The Kore complex: the myth and some unconscious fantasies. *International Journal of Psycho-Analysis* 75:243–263.

Ferguson, M. W. (1985). *Hamlet*: letters and spirits. In *Shakespeare and the Question of Theory*, ed. P. Parker and G. H. Hartman, pp. 292–309. New York: Methuen.

Ferrer, D. (1990). *Virginia Woolf and the Madness of Language*. London: Routledge.

Ficino, M. (1985). *Commentary on Plato's Symposium on Love*, tr. J. Sears. Dallas, TX: Spring Publications.

Foucault, M. (1985). *The Use of the Pleasure: Volume 2 of the History of Sexuality*. New York: Pantheon.

Freeman, B. (1986). Irigaray at the *Symposium*: speaking otherwise. *Oxford Literary Review* 8:170–177.

Friedländer, P. (1958). *Plato: An Introduction*, tr. H. Meyerhoff. New York: Pantheon.

Gallop, J. (1982). *The Daughter's Seduction: Feminism and Psychoanalysis*. Ithaca, NY: Cornell University Press.

Gilbert, S. (1986). Introduction. In *The Newly Born Woman*, ed. H. Cixous, and C. Clément, tr. B. Wing. Minneapolis: University of Minnesota Press.

Gilbert S., and Gubar, S. (1988). *No Man's Land. The Place of the Woman-Writer in the Twentieth Century.* Volume 1. *The War of the Words.* New Haven, CT: Yale University Press.

Godel, R. (1955). *Socrate et Diotime.* Paris: Les Belles Lettres.

Graham, J. (1990). Between the acts: the acts of interval. (unpublished manuscript).

Green, A. (1993). *Le Travail du negatif.* Paris: Minuit.

Grosz, E. (1989). *Sexual Subversions: Three French Feminists.* Sydney: Allen and Unwin.

Guthrie, W. K. C. (1986). *A History of Greek Philosophy.* Volume IV. *Plato. The Man and His Dialogues: Earlier Period.* Cambridge: Cambridge University Press.

Halperin, D. (1990). Why is Diotima a woman? In *One Hundred Years of Homosexuality*, pp. 113–151. New York: Routledge.

Harper, H. (1982). *Between Language and Silence: The Novels of Virginia Woolf.* Baton Rouge: Louisiana University Press.

Harvey, E. (1992). *Ventriloquized Voices: Feminist Theory and English Renaissance Texts.* London: Routledge.

Heidegger, M. (1961). *Nietzsche. Volume II: The Eternal Recurrence of the Same*, tr. D. F. Krell. San Francisco: Harper and Row, 1984.

Hesiod (1983). Theogony. Works and Days. Shield, tr. A. N. Athanassakis. Baltimore, MD: Johns Hopkins University Press.

Hesse H. (1943). *The Glass Bead Game. (Magister Ludi)*, tr. R. and C. Winston. London: Jonathan Cape, 1970.

Irigaray, L. (1992). *Elemental Passions*, tr. J. Collie and J. Still. New York: Routledge.

———— (1993). *An Ethics of Sexual Difference*, tr. C. Burke and G. C. Gill. Ithaca, NY: Cornell University Press.

Jacobus, M. (1986). *Reading Woman: Essays in Feminist Criticism.* New York: Columbia University Press.

Jardine, A. (1986). Opaque texts and transparent contexts: the political difference of Julia Kristeva, In *The Poetics of Gender*, ed. C. G. Heilbrun and N. K. Miller, pp. 96–116. New York: Columbia University Press.

Kirk, A. S. (1954). *Heraclitus: The Cosmic Fragments.* Cambridge: Cambridge University Press.

Kofman, S. (1983). *Comment s'en Sortir?* Paris: Galilée.

———— (1989). *Socrate(s).* Paris: Galilée.

Kristeva, J. (1969). *Recherches pour une sémanalyse.* (extraits). Paris: Seuil.

———— (1974). *La Révolution du langage poétique: l'avant-garde à la fin du XIXe siècle, Lautréamont et Mallarmé.* Paris: Seuil.

———— (1977). *Polylogue.* Paris: Seuil.

———— (1980). *Desire in Language: A Semiotic Approach to Literature and Art*, tr. T. Gora, A. Jardine, and L. S. Roudiez. New York: Columbia University Press.

———— (1981). Oscillation between power and denial. In *New French Feminisms*, ed. E. Marks and I. de Courtivron, pp. 165–167. New York: Schocken Books.

———— (1982). *Powers of Horror: An Essay on Abjection*, tr. L. S. Roudiez. New York: Columbia University Press.

———— (1983). Within the microcosm of the 'Talking Cure.' In *Interpreting Lacan*, ed. J. H. Smith and W. Kerrigan, pp. 33–48. New Haven: Yale University Press.

———— (1984). *Revolution in Poetic Language*, tr. M. Waller. New York: Columbia University Press.

———— (1986). *The Kristeva Reader*, ed. Toril Moi. New York: Columbia University Press.

———— (1987a). *In the Beginning Was Love: Psychoanalysis and Faith*, tr. A. Goldhammer. New York: Columbia University Press.

———— (1987b). *Tales of Love*, tr. L. S. Roudiez. New York: Columbia University Press.

———— (1989). *Black Sun: Depression and Melancholia*, tr. L. S. Roudiez. New York: Columbia University Press.

———— (1991). *Strangers to Ourselves*, tr. L. S. Roudiez. New York: Columbia University Press.

———— (1994). *Le Temps Sensible. Proust et l'Expérience Littéraire*. Paris: Gallimard.

———— (1995). Women's time. In *New Maladies of the Soul*, tr. R. Guberman. New York: Columbia University Press.

———— (1996). *Time and Sense: Proust and the Experience of Literature*, tr. R. Guberman. New York: Columbia University Press.

———— (2000a). *The Sense and Non-Sense of Revolt: The Powers and Limits of Psychoanalysis*. vol. I, tr. J. Herman. New York: Columbia University Press.

———— (2001a). *Hannah Arendt*, tr. R. Guberman. New York: Columbia University Press.

———— (2001b). *Melanie Klein*, tr. R. Guberman. New York: Columbia University Press.

———— (2001c). *Au Risque de la Pensée*. Paris: Édition de l'Aube.

———— (2002a). *Le Génie Féminin. Tome III. Colette ou la Chair du Monde*. Paris: Fayard.

———— (2002b). *La Langue, la Nation, les Femmes*. [*The Language, the Nation, the Women.*] Sofia: Sofia University Press.

Kristeva, J. et al. (1975). *La Traversée des signes*. Paris: Seuil.

Laurence, P. O. (1991). *The Reading of Silence: Virginia Woolf in the English Tradition*. Stanford: Stanford University Press.

Lechte, J. (1990). *Julia Kristeva*. London, New York: Routledge.

Lechte, J., and Zournazi, M., eds. (1998). *After The Revolution: On Kristeva*. Sydney: Artspace.

Levy, S. (1992). *Artificial Life: The Quest for a New Creation*. New York: Pantheon Books.

Lyotard, J.-F. (1984). *The Postmodern Condition: A Report on Knowledge*, tr. G. Bennington and B. Massumi. Minneapolis: University of Minnesota Press.

Miller, J. H. (1982). *Fiction and Repetition: Seven English Novels*. Cambridge: Harvard University Press.

Moi, T. (1985). *Sexual/Textual Politics: Feminist Literary Theory*. London and New York: Methuen.

Montaigne, M. (1948). *The Complete Works: Essays, Travel Journal, Letters*, tr. D. M. Frame. Stanford: Stanford University Press.

Morgan, M. L. (1990). *Platonic Piety: Philosophy and Ritual in Fourth-Century Athens*. New Haven and London: Yale University Press.

Mylonas, G. (1961). *Eleusis and the Eleusinian Mysteries*. Princeton: Princeton University Press.

Naremore, J. (1973). *The World Without a Self: Virginia Woolf and the Novel*. New Haven, CT: Yale University Press.

Neumann, H. (1965). Diotima's concept of love. *American Journal of Philology* 86: 33–59.

Nikolchina, M. (1992). *Chovekît-Utopiya*. [*The Utopian Human Being*.] Sofia: Sofia University Press.

Nussbaum, M. C. (1999). The Professor of parody: the hip defeatism of Judith Butler. *The New Republic*, February 22, pp. 37–45.

Oliver, K. (1993). *Reading Kristeva: Unraveling the Double-Bind*. Bloomington, IN: Indiana University Press.

Plato. (1953). Symposium. In *The Dialogues*, vol. 1., tr. B. Jowett, 4th. ed. Oxford: Clarendon.

———— (1988). *Phaedrus*, tr. C. J. Rowe, 2nd ed. Warminster: Aris and Phillips.

Rich, A. (1979). *On Lies, Secrets, and Silence*. New York: W. W. Norton.

Ricoeur, D. (1970). *Freud and Philosophy: An Essay on Interpretation*. New Haven and London: Yale University Press.

Robinson, T. M. (1987). *Heraclitus: Fragments. A Text and Translation with a Commentary*. Toronto: University of Toronto Press.

Rose, J. (1986). *Sexuality in the Field of Vision*. London: Verso NLB.

Rosen, S. (1968). *Plato's Symposium*. New Haven, CT, and London: Yale University Press.

Ruotolo, L. P. (1986). *The Interrupted Moment: A View of Virginia Woolf's Novels*. Stanford: Stanford University Press.

Schefold, K. (1943). *Die Bildnisse der Antiken Dichter, Redner und Denker*. Basel: Benno Schwabe.

Schiller, F. (1795). *On the Aesthetic Education of Man in a Series of Letters*, tr. E. M. Wilkinson and L. A. Willoughby. Oxford: Clarendon Press, 1967.

Schmid, W. (1987). *Die Geburt der Philosophie im Garten der Lüste: Michael Foucault's Archäologie des platonischen Eros*. [*The Birth of Philosophy in the Garden of De-*

sire: Michael Foucault's Archeology of the Platonic Eros.] Frankfurt am Main: Athenäum.

Schopenhauer, A. (1819). *The World as Will and Representation*, tr. E. F. J. Payne, vol. I. New York: Dover, 1969.

Scott, J. (2001). Fantasy echo: history and the construction of identity. *Critical Inquiry* 27(Winter):284–304.

——— (2002). Feminist reverberations. *Differences* 13:3.

Shelley, M. (1818). *Frankenstein or, the Modern Prometheus*. Oxford: Oxford University Press, 1969.

Showalter, E. (1977). *A Literature of Their Own: British Women Novelists from Brontë to Lessing*. Princeton: Princeton University Press.

——— (1999). *A Literature of Their Own: British Women Novelists from Brontë to Lessing*, expanded edition. Princeton: Princeton University Press.

Silver, B. R. (1979). "Anon" and the "Reader": Virginia Woolf's Last Essays. *Twentieth Century Literature* 25(Fall/Winter):356–441.

——— (1989). Retro-anger and baby-boomer nostalgia: a polemical talk. *Virginia Woolf and Her Influences: Selected Papers from the Seventh Annual Conference on Virginia Woolf*, ed. L. Davis and J. McVicker. New York: Pace University Press.

Silverman, K. (1988). *The Acoustic Mirror: The Female Voice in Psychoanalysis and Film*. Bloomington, IN: Indiana University Press.

Smith, A. (1996). *Julia Kristeva: Readings of Exile and Estrangement*. New York: St. Martin's Press.

Spivak, G. C. (1988). *In Other Worlds: Essays in Cultural Politics*. New York: Routledge.

Stanton, D. C. (1986). Difference on trial: a critique of the maternal metaphor in Cixous, Irigaray, and Kristeva. In *The Poetics of Gender*, ed. C. G. Heilbrun and N. K. Miller, pp. 157–182. New York: Columbia University Press.

Taylor, A. E. (1963). *Plato: The Man and His Work*. London: Methuen.

Warner, E., ed. (1984). *Virginia Woolf: A Centenary Perspective*. London: Macmillan.

Wellmer, A. (1991). *The Persistence of Modernity. Essays on Aesthetics, Ethics, and Postmodernism*, tr. D. Midgley. Cambridge, MA: MIT Press.

Whitford, M. (1991). *Luce Irigaray: Philosophy in the Feminine*. London: Routledge.

——— (1994). Reading Irigaray in the nineties. In *Engaging with Irigaray: Feminist Philosophy and Modern European Thought*, ed. C. Burke, N. Schor, and M. Whitford. New York: Columbia University Press.

Wieland, C. (2000). *The Undead Mother: Psychoanalytic Explorations of Masculinity, Femininity, and Matricide*. London: Rebus Press.

Wilamowitz-Moellendorff, U. (1920). *Platon: Leben und Werke*. Erster Band. Berlin: Weidmannsche Buchhandlung.

Wollstonecraft, M. (1979). *The Collected Letters*, ed. R. M. Wardle. Ithaca, NY: Cornell University Press.

Woolf, V. (1912–1922). *The Letters of Virginia Woolf*, vol. II, ed. N. Nicolson. New York: Harcourt Brace Jovanovich, 1976.

—— (1915). *The Voyage Out*. London: Hogarth Press, 1957.

—— (1925a). *Mrs. Dalloway*. London, Penguin, 1992.

—— (1925b). On not knowing Greek. *The Common Reader*, 5th ed., pp. 39–59. London: Hogarth Press, 1945.

—— (1927). *To the Lighthouse*. London: Penguin, 1973.

—— (1931). *The Waves*. New York: Harcourt.

—— (1935). *A Room of One's Own*. London: Hogarth.

—— (1938). *Three Guineas*. London: Hogarth, 1986.

—— (1941). *Between the Acts*. London: Penguin, 1974.

—— (1942). *The Death of the Moth and Other Essays*. London: Hogarth.

—— (1944). An unwritten novel. In *A Haunted House*. London: Penguin, 1973.

—— (1953). *A Writer's Diary*, ed. Leonard Woolf. London: Triad Grafton, 1987.

—— (1958). Women and fiction. In *Granite and Rainbow*, pp. 76–84. London: Hogarth.

—— (1985). *Moments of Being*, ed. J. Schulkind, 2nd ed. London: Hogarth, 1985.

Wyatt, J. (1978). The Celebration of Eros: Greek concepts of love and beauty. In *To the Lighthouse*. *Philosophy and Literature* 2:160–175.

Index